A Spectacular Catastrophe

and other things I recommend

Copyright © 2017 Dushka Zapata

All rights reserved

ISBN: 1545144346

ISBN-13: 978-1545144343

Cover image courtesy of Freepik.com

There is a crack

A crack

In everything

That's how the light gets in.

— Leonard Cohen

Boyfriend, this one's for you.

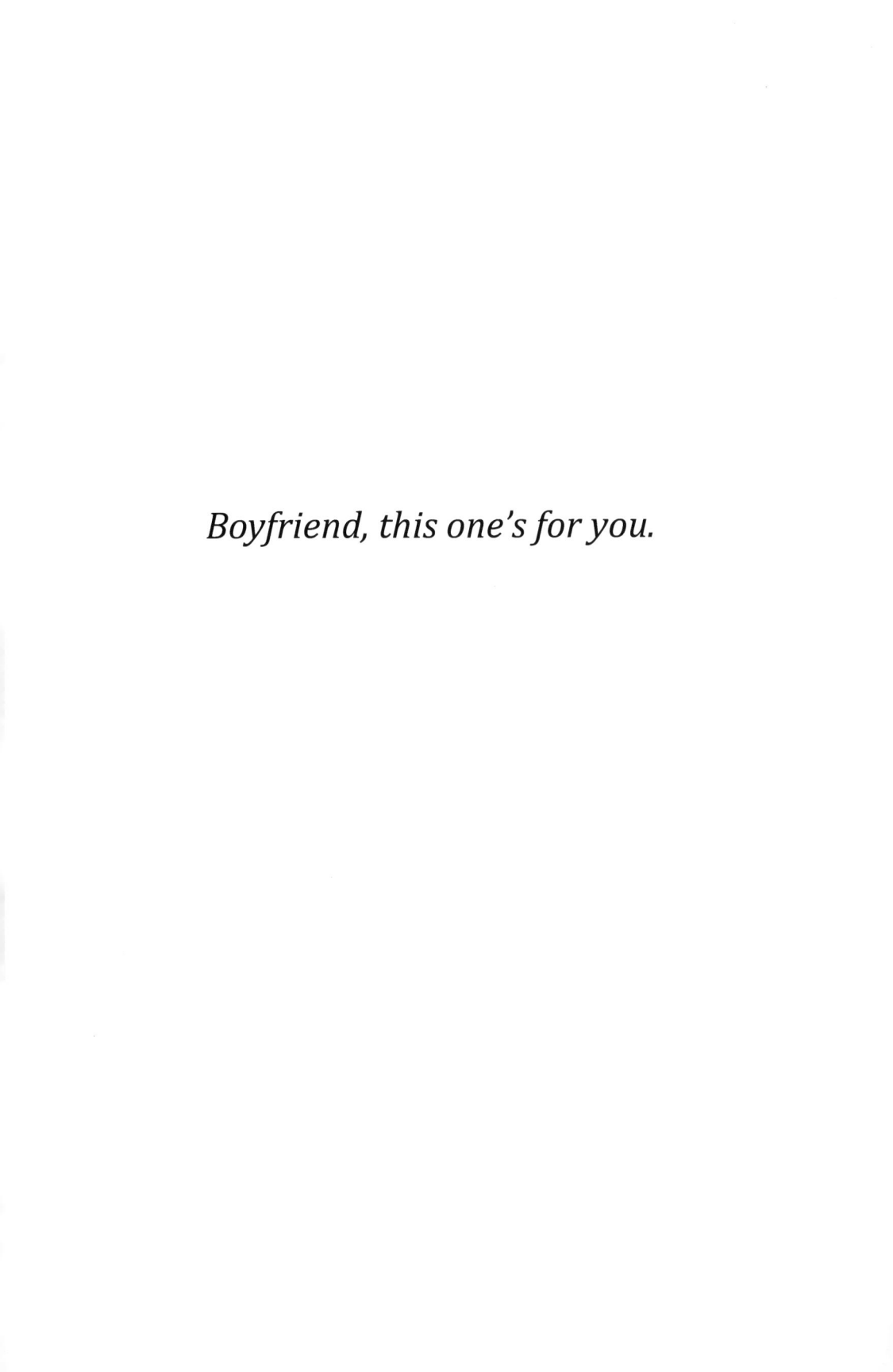

Author's Note:

Any reference to time across the book ("a month ago, a week ago") respects when the essay was written.

Contents

But First, Love Yourself	1
How To Let Go	3
Everything Is A Habit	5
Don't Make It True	6
Identical Routine	8
Spectacular Catastrophe	10
If You Are Sad, Be Sad	12
Anxiety	14
Don't Look Now	16
What To Do When Someone Lies To You	17
How To Write A Book	19
Retroactive Jealousy	21
Here. Now.	22
Why Silence Is So Important	23
Inner Entanglement	25
Nothing By Force	26
Interruptions	27

Start Here	29
Left Out	31
A Single Puzzle	33
What You Seek Is Seeking You—Rumi	35
Tethered	37
I Love You/I Need You	38
Pain/Suffering	39
How To Fix A Broken Heart	41
Boundaries: A Moving Target	42
Obstacles To Writing	45
An Option	47
I Don't Know What I Want	49
The Cure For Pain	51
Cost Of Admission	53
The Good People	54
An Enjoyable Thing	56
My Puppy Heart	58
Don't Chase The Pain	60
I Command Me	61

It's My Name	63
To Improve Your Vocabulary	64
Crush	66
The Most Powerful Tool	67
Being Single	69
Things I've Thrown Out	70
"Some Day" Will Never Be Today	71
Struggle	73
Counterintuitive Life Lessons	74
Resentment	76
Repetition	77
The Virtue In Indecision	79
Detachment	80
Happiness Is Elusive	82
Your Constant Reminder	84
How To Suffer Less	85
Plaits And Spirals	87
Restlessness	88
Introverts And Parties	90

Sanskara	92
Brutal Honesty	94
Laundry Zen	96
Your Regard For Yourself	97
An Alternative	99
Arm Balances	101
After A Break Up	102
How To Be Less Boring	104
Midlife Crisis	105
The Most Beautiful Thing	107
Male For A Day	108
The Meaning Of Words	110
Everyone Is In A Bad Mood	112
Gut Instinct	113
How To Get Your Shit Together	115
Why Do We Misunderstand Each Other?	117
The Best	119
People Pleaser	120
Stand There And Take It	122

Things To Let Go Of	123
How To Be A Good Friend	124
Transference	126
Mindfulness/Flow	128
Worry	129
Advice For Women (or anyone)	130
Instructions On What To See	131
Love At Thirteen	133
How To Screw Up Your Life	135
Trigger	136
Go Somewhere	137
Lack Of Trust	139
How To Stop Taking Things Personally	140
Advisor	142
Different From Me	144
Blind Spot	146
Being Yourself	147
Disinterested Friend	148
The Best Of Me	150

How To Feel More Grateful	151
Increased Responsibility	153
What Is It Like To Have No Control?	155
How Did My Parents' Divorce Affect Me?	157
The Moon And The Stars	158
Shapeshifting Is Not A Superpower	160
Where Are All The Good Guys?	161
Possessed	162
Being Honest Versus Complaining	163
Ultimatum	164
Small Decisions	165
An Invisible Prison	166
Is Ego Good Or Bad?	167
You Can't Miss Out If You're Doing Exactly What You Want	169
Please Change For Me	171
How To Conquer Fear	173
How Do Lovers Who Speak Different Languages Understand Each Other?	174
The Jungle That Is My Brain	176
Alternate Reality	178

Your Inner Hero	179
I Wish I'd Known This Sooner	180
Curiosity	182
A Healthy Relationship	183
Irrational Terror	185
Ground Rules	187
Good People/Bad People	188
Love At First Sight	189
Don't Slap A Child	191
Why Breakups Hurt	192
Truth And Fact	194
Loyalty, Misguided	195
So Curvy	197
Hold The Mirror	198
Looking In The Right Place	199
Who Holds The Power In Your Relationship?	200
Other Things I Recommend	201
How To Be Asked Out	202
Open	203

Emotionally Dependent/In Love	204
How To Keep The People That You Love	205
Don't Be A Thief	207
Lose Yourself/Find Yourself	208
Cassandra's Curse	210
Relationship History	211
Is That Really True?	212
Please Love Me, Please Leave Me	214
The Wrong Filter	216
Alone	218
Does The Universe Conspire In My Favor?	220
Playing It Safe/Being A Coward	222
Only You	223
Online Dating—Off To A Good Start	225
Meditation	226
Misnomer	228
Save Yourself Some Time	229
Empathy/Compassion	230
Never Stop Learning	232

Thank You, Quora	233
Baby Dragons	235
Trust Your Feet	237
Comparing Myself To Others	239
Unlikely Skill	240
Beautiful	242
Be A Baby	243
Do Me	245
How To Be An Optimist	246
The Crook Of My Arm	248
How To Change Your Outlook	250
Treasure Hunt	252
We Create What Destroys Us	254
Why Life Is Not A Movie	255
Life-Long Exercise	256
Needed	258
Leap Of Faith	259
Rainbow	260
Should You Push Yourself To Write?	261

How To Get Over Being Cheated On	262
How To Solve A Problem	264
How To Deal With Someone Better Than You	266
Should I Ask My Crush Why She Stares At Me?	267
It's A System	268
"Easy" Is A Decoy	270
How To Explain Divorce To A Kid	271
Bad At It	273
Please Don't Save Me	274
Comebacks	276
Narcissism/Self Love	277
Up The Ante	279
Cheer Up!	281
Overactive Imagination	283
Another Example Of A Spectacular Catastrophe	285
Don't Bother	287
How To Be A Good Stepmother	289
Maybe It's Not About You	291
Rumination	293

It's Me I'm Angry At	294
Incompatible	295
Change The Record	297
When I Was Thirteen	298
Later Will Be Better	300
Vulnerability/Neediness	302
How To Be Sure You Are Marrying The Right Person	303
Echo Chambers	305
Real Threat	307
A Storm Is Coming	309
Distant Planets	310
Remind Yourself	312
My Indestructible Heart	314
Everyone's Fine	315
Tease	317
Time Is Running Out	319
Good Questions To Ask The First Time You Meet Someone	321
Listen To Your Feelings	322
Don't Work Too Hard	324

Pedestal	326
Are You The One Who Is Toxic?	327
Trust Is For You	328
Why Do We Make Life Complicated?	329
You Don't Have To Live Like This	330
Regret	332
Ego/Self-Esteem	333
Expectations	334
Why Does No Mean Yes?	335
My Internal Ocean	337
Happy Doesn't Just Happen	339
How Important Is A Partner With Ambition?	340
Farmer's Market	341
Toxic Relationships Can Be Turned Around	343
Nobody Cares	345
Go Make Something	347
Your Puzzle	349
Morning Person	350

But First, Love Yourself

I am hypersensitive to being a burden on others.

A few nights ago, I asked a friend to give me a ride to my house (normally I walk but it was rainy and later than usual) and she hesitated for a split second.

I immediately told her *"Please don't worry. I can just call a cab."*

"But, why?" she said.

"I really don't want to put you out" I said. *"Calling a cab is no problem at all."*

"But, where did you get that idea? I would be so happy to give you a ride. You live less than 6 minutes away. I was just thinking about something else when you asked me."

Me feeling like I was making her uncomfortable had nothing to do with her and everything to do with me.

In a million big and small ways we project who we are onto others.

If you don't love yourself, you can love others. Except that not loving yourself alters your perception, disfiguring everything: who you are attracted to, why you decide to stay, your boundaries.

You ask questions like this: *Why do I give everything when I receive nothing? Why does every man I date treat me poorly? Why does every relationship I have end with the man cheating on me? Why are all men emotionally unavailable? Why are all men scum?*

If you don't love yourself, the way you love will be distorted by the fact that you don't believe you deserve to be loved.

How To Let Go

I think I was in my early twenties when it hit me that a human being cannot own another.

It felt so much like we belonged to each other but the fact is that despite our peculiar tendency to want to relinquish ourselves we can never stop being free.

Contrary to those who claim to know another well, we are not unfailingly predictable. We do surprising things to reclaim our glorious, frightening sovereignty.

Behold. Behold its splendor.

Despite one thousand promises the person who has sworn is mine and will be forever can (gasp) leave any day. He can change his mind or have a change of heart.

He can very quickly recover should I be the one to decide to leave.

He can move forward and begin another life, identical to the one he had with me, only with someone new.

Or a completely different one, going from utterly familiar to unrecognizable.

We declare undying love yet carry within something feral that refuses to be completely possessed.

This is why we need to love well and respectfully and take nothing for granted.

No one owns us and we move on and this is our salvation.

It turns out I never needed to worry about when to "let go" of someone. I didn't "have them." I never did.

Everything Is A Habit

Nearly everything is a habit.

If you think you like junk food and don't like vegetables, start eating well and you'll lose your taste for junk food. Vegetables will begin to taste good. They will be what you crave.

What you think is taste is habit.

If you cannot imagine letting go of crippling things like worry and guilt, realize that you inadvertently practice and reinforce both those things every day and, as such, you can practice replacing thoughts of worry with better thoughts.

What you think is in your nature is habit.

If you are haunted by jealousy, know you feed it with your obsessive thinking and your paranoia. Feed love. Feed trust in yourself. Your jealousy will shrink until you can't remember why you ever felt that way.

They are not shortcomings. They are habits.

To me, realizing that my flaws are habits that I can have an impact on—even if getting there from here seems impossible—coupled with the fact that given enough practice I can do a lot of things I previously thought I couldn't well.

We are never powerless.

Don't Make It True

I am in the middle of an intensive training to become a yoga teacher.

Today in class we realized most of us asked the same question before we started.

Can you guess what it is?

I would like to take this training but I worry I am not right for it because I am too young.

...because I am too old.

...because I am not flexible.

...because I cannot get into advanced poses.

...because I haven't done yoga for long enough.

Do you know what makes a good yoga teacher? Among other things, an understanding of what makes people human. You have to teach from your own experience. You cannot teach without empathy.

We all tell ourselves that we are not right for what we love. That we fall short. That someone is out of our league.

Let me tell you something I have learned about myself that is true about you too because it's true about everyone.

You are enough.

These lies we reinforce by repeating them over and over (*I am an impostor*) make no sense. They are not true.

But we can make them true.

If I believe myself when I say with relentless tenacity that I am not enough, I will set into action a self fulfilling prophecy that will go like this:

I believe I am not good enough and therefore will sow insecurity into my heart.

I will cheat myself out of opportunities. I will fail at something before I begin.

I will become jealous and possessive of the person that I love.

I will try to control him to avoid losing him.

Every action will become evidence that he is planning to leave me.

And he will.

Not because I am not good enough but because I will drive him insane with my insecure delusions.

Learn to love yourself before you drive away the people that you love.

Identical Routine

You decide you are going to run every day.

You map out a route to follow every morning. It starts flat, has hills, a curve, a park, then the home stretch. It takes around 40 minutes.

You set the alarm for the same time and the loop never varies, but every day is completely different.

That hill sure feels steeper today, doesn't it? And the park, normally placid, frustrates you. How slow everyone is moving, the obstructions in your path.

This isn't because the route is different, but because you are.

You see your inner fluctuations more clearly because they stand out against the backdrop of an identical routine.

Some days a flare of anger appears out of nowhere and ignites in your chest.

Some days you run liked the winged goddess of victory.

Some days you want a shortcut. You think about skipping the hill.

Some days you want to skip the run.

Will you?

What do you do when no one is watching but you, when this matters to no one but you?

What will you discover about yourself two weeks in, seven months in, two years in?

What insight will reveal itself? What knot will you untangle?

Who are you?

Routine is valuable because you remove distractions and excuses.

It's where you go to meet yourself.

Spectacular Catastrophe

One of the hardest things to do is to not believe everything you think.

It means the person you need to doubt is yourself.

It means you have to be open, open to the possibility you are wrong.

And often it means embarking on the challenging exercise of un-believing what you were once convinced of.

Once you un-believe, things tend to unravel. Implode. Fall apart.

Bringing on this spectacular catastrophe is the only way to be truly happy.

Our unhappiness relies on our beliefs. Challenge your belief, shake your unhappiness.

Example: I believed for years in the purity and beauty of unconditional love.

I can do this. I am the one who can love you unconditionally.

But unconditional love means the other person can do anything. Be despicable. Hurt you. Step all over you. Take you for granted.

What if this thing that I was always told was poetry was instead a fallacy, a lie, like your soul mate, like love at first sight, like the notion of finding your purpose?

I don't love anyone unconditionally. And I don't believe everything anyone thinks. Not even myself. In particular not myself.

I owe myself that.

If You Are Sad, Be Sad

I woke up sad today. A dark weight on my chest. It feels like I have something to drag behind me when I would rather walk sprightly, unburdened.

I could ignore it but when I ignore feelings they seem to assemble inside me and plot and prepare for war.

They make strategic plans to present themselves before me all at once at the worst possible moments.

I really don't want to burst out crying in the middle of a presentation.

I don't want to fight with Boyfriend over something that doesn't matter.

I do what I always do when I have feelings I need to sort out.

I set time aside to do nothing.

So, what is this? I have felt this way before.

Finally it hits me. My father died in December. I don't immediately associate the date with the anniversary of his death but my body does.

And today is December 1st.

I could fill my days with work and friends and fake holiday cheer to distract me from myself but as counterintuitive as it might seem I'm just going to stay home and be sad.

Feelings, like waves, relentless, powerful, intractable, need space to arrive and swell and retreat.

I have learned it's much better to give them what they need.

Anxiety

My brain is so frustratingly noisy.

In particular before a trip back home.

"I need to pack make sure I don't forget anything check my email reply to that text did I throw the wet clothes in the drier I haven't had breakfast need to toss the towels in the wash the windows are they closed"

Wait a minute.

"Hey! Thoughts! Listen up!

"You all need to settle down! I know you are trying to help but you are all over the place! You are overwhelming me! I can't finish a single thing! I feel so anxious right now ack!

"I'm going to sit down and take three slow deep breaths over here and then focus on one thing only, OK? I have to pack with my full attention because otherwise we will all end up at the airport without our passport."

I pack. I try to enjoy the process, lovingly fold things, assemble my clothes harmoniously in my carry-on.

Nothing else will get done while I do this but nothing at all was getting done before when I was prey to my own flitting mental impulses.

I might set down the dress I'm folding and note what I'm doing this for.

"Hey. I know traveling back home is really stressful for you but think about how lucky you are to hang out with mom.

"Thank you. Thank you for doing what matters the most."

I've been trying to practice for a while stopping the chatter by noticing it, asking everyone to pipe down while I breathe and identify the truly important thing, and then doing only that and enjoying it.

Saying thank you for it.

Thank you for so much good fortune.

Has this calmed my noisy brain, its distressed, distracting, panicked, scattered voices?

Do I feel better, more grounded and present?

Some days.

On the days it's freaking out I round everyone up, ask that they pipe down and begin again.

Don't Look Now

One of my yoga teachers likes to dedicate his entire class to building up to a final, complex pose.

He does related poses and stretches and by the end everyone is warm and pliable and elastic and ready to attempt something new, or at least ready to get a bit closer to an unlikely pose becoming possible.

He says that once he explains the asana everyone has been working up to he sees an ocean of beautiful, sweaty, contorted faces holding this new pose in perfect alignment while simultaneously saying *"But there is no way I can do this!"*

Don't look now, but you might already be doing many things you think you can't.

What To Do When Someone Lies To You

I detest lies.

I detest lies so much I was quick to sever contact with anyone who lied to me.

Then, someone very, very important to me lied.

I tried to bring down my strict rule swiftly and the thought of casting this person out of my life brought me to my knees.

So I walked over to the mirror and I looked at myself right in the eye.

Tell me. It's just you and me here.

Do I always tell the truth?

And she knew.

Can I hold someone else up to standards I don't comply with?

And then I asked her a more difficult question.

With these high principles of yours, with your tendency to fight so righteously, do you sometimes put people who love you in a position where lying is just easier than fighting?

I cannot continue to judge those close to me as if I was beyond reproach.

I cannot change another person but I can look at the role I play in how things turn out.

I am not talking about lowering my expectations of love. I am talking about the need to recognize that others are human, and soften, soften my demands so they wrap around reality in a way that makes life more viable.

Here are other questions that I asked me that day.

Why are you trying so hard to "catch" the person you are supposed to trust?

Why is someone hiding things that might be innocent?

Could it be because they are tired of fights you know are unreasonable?

And what happens if I leave him and then replicate this pattern in every relationship—because I will—*and one day realize that I really want to stay but have trapped myself into a corner?*

I think lack of trust will pretty much do a relationship in. And I detest lies, in particular when they are about seemingly innocuous things.

But life is not always that simple and if you are an active participant in this dynamic it will catch up to you.

And by "you" I of course mean me.

How To Write A Book

I often feel completely overwhelmed.

Sometimes I sit down and pull out a notebook and make a list of all the things I have to do just to identify what is making me feel this way.

The answer is never on the list.

What makes me feel overwhelmed is the (false) impression that I have to get everything done right now.

Then I read this Einstein quote:

"Time exists so that everything doesn't happen at once."

I took in what my mom tells me every time she sees me biting off more than I can chew.

"One day at a time, Dushka. Take it one day at a time."

I didn't ever write a book or even a chapter. I wrote a page at a time and relished every bit.

Before I knew it that became my first book, and then it became my second. This one is my third.

"One day at a time", beyond book writing, is sound advice for anything that feels daunting or unattainable.

Turns out, there is no such thing.

This notion never fails to reduce my angst over all the things I'm not getting done.

Retroactive Jealousy

The angriest I have ever been at Boyfriend was because of a relationship that took place before he met me.

I wanted him to go back to his past and change it. Delete it. Delete all of it.

This is not only impossible, it's irrational.

I locked myself up in the bathroom and raged.

This proved highly ineffective.

So I looked within me. And worked at figuring out what my stories were, exactly what my insecurities are and where they come from.

Because most of the times that I am mad at someone else my anger is related to my own history.

If I feel jealous, I acknowledge my feelings and set them down where they belong.

Hello again, kind, devastating monster.

I see you.

Thank you for trying to protect me.

You can go now.

Here. Now.

Chasing my thoughts is the opposite of being present. It's a form of sleepwalking, paying attention to nothing, enjoying nothing, being yanked around by things inside my brain that are largely insignificant.

Presence is about waking up to the fact that I'm doing this and opening my eyes to what is before me. How beautiful this moment is and how I don't really need to plan for the next one.

You can be always be present. To your morning, to your coffee, to traffic, to the people in your life.

Presence is about less. Less noise. Less mind-chatter. Less angst.

More now.

Why Silence Is So Important

A few days ago a construction crew was fixing a pothole right below my apartment. The noise was hellacious. I couldn't hear myself think.

Noise is probably the thing that drains me the most. I feel my energy leaking out of me, my precious life force replaced by pure irritation and frazzle and an urge to get out.

Get me out of here.

The world is a noisy place. It's the honking and clanging and banging and drilling.

But it's also the words.

Everyone has an opinion on what I should be, could be, shouldn't be doing. I hear suggestions all day long.

No wonder I lose track of who I am, what I want and what I need to do. I can hear others loud and clear again and again but I can't hear myself.

No wonder I feel lost. No wonder I feel disoriented.

I have a guide but I can't hear her.

I am then bombarded by messages that I am not enough. I need to do more, work harder, be busier and more productive. I need to buy something, get something, change something.

And I need to hurry, because what I need is running out.

No wonder I feel inadequate. No wonder I'm convinced everything is scarce.

Don't you see? Scarcity sells.

The antidote to all of this madness is silence.

If I sit in a quiet corner for a while, my energy trickles back. I can hear myself again. I can hear me, who I am, what I want. I realize I am enough. I have enough. I don't need anything other than what I already am.

Silence lets the Truth right in.

Inner Entanglement

My father was powerful and authoritative and strong and fiercely protective.

This may or may not be why I am particularly adverse to anyone attempting to tell me what to do.

But, wait. If only it was that simple.

It also may or may not be why if someone did not try to control me or possess me I felt they did not love me.

You can see how this combination made it unlikely for me to develop a relationship that wasn't dysfunctional.

I could look far and I could look wide but until I didn't address this inner entanglement I wouldn't stand a chance.

I began healing dysfunctional relationships as I began to look more clearly at myself.

Nothing By Force

I have very tight hamstrings. I can't tell you how much this bothers me. This tightness has an impact on my lower back and I am usually stiff and in pain, in particular because I spend so much of my time sitting at a computer.

I am in a yoga class attempting to stretch out through a seated forward fold. I feel the familiar frustration at my inability to gently and gracefully rest my forehead on my legs.

Aaaaaarg.

This frustration makes my body clench.

Which in turn makes me tighter.

I want to thrash but instead take deep breaths. Inhale. Exhale.

My hamstrings loosen and I come down a tiny bit more.

This exercise teaches me so much. That nothing is accomplished through force. That tantrums are not efficient. That I cannot approach everything as if I was in a battle, in particular with myself.

That relaxing, however counterintuitive, can often be more effective.

That I need to accept myself the way I am. I will never fold over my legs, and that is perfectly OK.

Yoga. The perfect metaphor for life.

Interruptions

The great annihilator of writing is being interrupted.

There you are, words swirling around you poised to line up and come out of your fingers and someone approaches you and—

Gone. They are gone.

"Hey, can I interrupt you just for quick a second?"

Thwacks forehead against table.

Being interrupted is an inspiration assassin, and yet not quite the biggest challenge.

The biggest challenge is how to not allow my brain to interrupt itself.

Once I have stepped out of the world, carved out some time alone, set everything up to allow for harmony, quiet and concentration, then what happens?

Dushka, ick. You really need to wash the pots and pans soaking in the sink.

You haven't gone to the supermarket and the fridge is empty.

You still owe that client the follow up document.

Have you called your mom?

The challenge is to push all these things aside to write.

The sparking swirl of words is demanding, fragile, spontaneous, capricious. It doesn't appear when you invite it. It comes when it's good and ready.

Without a deliberate, regular, intentional effort to make space for it and protect it both from others and from yourself, the swirl will disappear and (at least in that same order) will not return.

Start Here

I ran into a friend a few days ago and was so very happy to see her.

We usually hug each other tight but this time she seemed to be someplace else.

I briefly wondered if she might be irked at me. I ran through my mind what had taken place the last time I saw her.

I couldn't think of anything. It bugged me.

I found out this morning that when I saw her she was dealing with a family emergency.

She had been indeed somewhere else, for reasons that had nothing to do with me.

There was a story I inadvertently fabricated, and then there was what was actually going on.

Between my story and hers, a gap.

What is that?

What is that space that lies between the assumptions that we make and what is actually happening?

It's dangerous, that space. It creates most misunderstandings.

It separates us from every one of our relationships, even the one we have with reality.

What would it take to narrow that space, to some day obliterate it forever?

This is what I would start with.

Left Out

A good friend of Boyfriend's organized a party tonight and I didn't want to go.

But.

As it often happens, a lot of my friends would be there and Boyfriend was excited about going so I decided I'd get over myself and rally.

When I arrived I realized the group was bigger than I expected. The party was at a bar and it was noisy.

I made an effort to go around talking to those I wanted to see but I find that at parties people want to chat in groups rather than one on one.

This simply does not lead to the conversations I am interested in having—more intimate, I guess.

I feel awkward, get restless, frustrated, isolated.

At one point (probably 45 minutes in) my brain stepped in.

"GET OUT. I NEED TO GET OUT."

So I called a cab and came home.

I walked around my house feeling dismayed and left out (To be honest I leave myself out because all my friends are welcoming and have gotten used to my introversion attacks).

Why can't I like parties?

Why can't I loosen up and enjoy the company of the people I like?

I tidy up my house, fold some clothes, wipe the kitchen counter. It would appear I'm cleaning my apartment but really I'm sorting out my insides.

I cut up an apple and bring my plate in front of my computer.

And here we are.

I feel everything begin to right itself. It's quiet here, my brain winds down and I'm home.

It's less lonely here with me.

The trick is to embrace who I am rather than try to push myself to be something I'm not.

No one is leaving me out. I'm just different, and as hard as that can be sometimes I can assure you it's a gift.

A Single Puzzle

I can recite by heart poems I learned in elementary school.

If I read something beautiful I remember how aesthetic and architectural the sentences looked on the page.

If another writer expresses something I didn't even know I felt, the words are like spirals that coil their way into my chest, inextricable.

I remember clear as day their structure and the order they were in and if they were on the left side or the right side of the page.

I recall the page number.

I find it near impossible to fill out a form. I see blank spaces that demand my information and it's like I can't even remember my name.

When I had to provide a signature to a lawyer in relation to my father's last will, I signed with flourish in the wrong space. *"Dushka!"* My brother said in complete exasperation. *"You had one job."*

If at a restaurant I have to walk to the bathroom I get lost on the way back to my table. I use my navigation system to return home from running an errand at the corner store.

Our brains are different and what seems second nature to you is near impossible to another.

Sometimes I wonder if we are all supposed to be a team working together to solve a single puzzle that requires every one of us to be successfully completed.

What You Seek Is Seeking You
—Rumi

Whenever I try to decode a concept I can't fully grasp I begin by looking for the most simple answer.

To use medical slang for arriving at a diagnosis, *"When you hear hoof beats, think horses, not zebras."*

Let's say that somewhere in San Francisco a talented baker is making blueberry pie with the intent to sell this brilliant concoction.

Naturally, this dessert creator would like to find someone who'd want to buy this pie.

At the same time, I'm sitting in my apartment and it's mid-afternoon. I consider (because it's an excellent idea) venturing outside for a cup of coffee and a slice of blueberry pie.

What I am looking for is looking for me.

I love to write for its own sake, but I also like thinking someone out there finds what I write useful.

Maybe there is someone who is waiting for my answers at the same time that I'm hoping there is someone who will read them.

Hello?

Is anybody there?

Oh, hi.

If you are looking to read what I write, then I can assure you what you're looking for is looking for you.

And here we are, writer and reader together at last.

Now, aside from writing and reading and pie, can one extrapolate this principle into everything?

At the very least it's worth pondering and being bewitched by it.

And that's what makes it beautiful.

Tethered

I am afraid of emptiness. A void.

When I'm in a car and there is a pronounced curve or decline I have this irrational sensation that the vehicle I'm in will detach from the road and fall up into the sky.

At night when I'm trying to sleep I'm kept up by this same impression, that what glues my body to my bed is precarious and friable.

It helps to sleep with something heavy on my chest, like a sandbag or Boyfriend's big arm draped over me.

When I grieve what I feel most besides fear is a sense of becoming unmoored.

I need to be tethered to something.

I realized that to avoid this sensation or to be able to live with it I couldn't carry sandbags everywhere I went.

I needed to count on myself, to be solid enough to become my own anchor.

I am my dock.

It's me I'm tethered to, and that's how I know I can deal with uncertainty.

I Love You/I Need You

Feelings that identify wanting to be with someone:
Genuine interest in the other person
Desire for their happiness, even when it doesn't involve you
Balanced, rewarding relationship
Serenity and comfort when you are alone
Ability and interest in doing other things

Feelings that identify desperation:
Clingy
Needy
Dependent
Grasping
Controlling
Dramatic
Wanting to be with the person every minute of every day
Inability to do things that do not involve him (or her)
A desire for them to do badly without you
Anxiety when you are alone.

Pain/Suffering

A few months ago I went to LA for work. I spent a couple of nights at a modern, sleek hotel. My room was enormous and glossy and made me feel it was much cooler than me (I mean this as a compliment to both of us).

Right by the bed there was this white leather lounge chair that had oddly angled metal legs.

I knew right away they were trouble.

I got up in the middle of the night to jaunt to the bathroom and thwacked my toe on that oddly angled metal leg. It hurt so much I thought I'd pass out. (No such luck. I had to stay lucid and moan.)

I hopped over to the white tiled restroom in the dark and the floor felt sticky.

I turned the light on and realized I was leaving bloody footprints across the bathroom floor.

Oh my God I broke my toe and will need stitches and won't make it to my training tomorrow I won't be able to do yoga for months I wonder if I need a hospital I am here all alone

My toe was throbbing. That's pain.

My brain thought we were experiencing a massive crisis of far-reaching consequences. That's suffering.

We're going to be OK (You have to be very firm with a freaked out brain). *We will jump in the shower, rinse the blood off and gently assess the damage. Then we will make some decisions.*

I will spare you the details of how my toe looked but I will say that, despite the carnage, things worked out much better than my brain anticipated.

This is frequently the case: many, many of the things that make us suffer end up being no more than stories we tell ourselves.

How To Fix A Broken Heart

There is no fix.

I don't think I ever heal from a broken heart.

It doesn't set back to the way it was.

The only way for my heart to grow—to expand—is for it to break. Because after it has been broken I develop a new perspective—a new understanding.

Heartbreak is the only way to develop true empathy and compassion.

Boundaries: A Moving Target

It's Saturday morning. The alarm goes off early because Boyfriend wants to go to the gym. Instead of moving back so he can get up, I burrow. *"Snuggle me for one minute"* I say.

I go to a coffee shop to meet a friend. It's pretty crowded and I ask a couple if they are willing to share their table. Most of the time the answer is yes but sometimes they tell me they are having a private conversation. *"Would you mind terribly sitting somewhere else?"*

From there I go to my three hour anatomy course. It's part of my ongoing yoga education. We're here to learn proper alignment. Finding what works for each body means more comfort, less struggle, less risk of injury.

This means I touch people. I put my hands on their temples, their neck, their shoulders. I wrap my fingers around their hips, the soles of their feet.

In this environment, touch is expected. When we teach in a yoga studio we have to be direct and specific. *"If you don't want to be touched tell me now."*

If a fellow student were to approach me and slide his hands over me, salaciously rather than clinically, I would step back and say no.

Intent changes who can touch me and how.

I see a friend in child's pose and go over and make a common adjustment to help release her lower back. I place the palms of my hand over the base of her spine and add my weight. Then I slide my hands up over the length of her back and squeeze her neck. I'm not caressing. It's a transaction. *"Yeeeees. Oh my god, thank you."* she says.

I'm meeting a friend for dinner and I always try to get away from having to drive. *"Can you pick me up?"* I ask. It's a bit out of her way. *"Normally I'd say yes but I'm tight on time. Can we meet there?"*

I spend my days testing and pushing people's boundaries. We all do. We don't know what they are because they vary per individual, moment by moment, with our own intention, and probably with the weather and other unspecified meteorological conditions.

I also test and push people's boundaries because I try to make my world more convenient for me. I suppose I'm often selfish, on the grounds that I'm human. We want what we want, and we negotiate to get it.

I am constantly weighing my own boundaries. It's extremely difficult. They are a moving target.

Some mornings I don't want to snuggle. The request for an extra minute, made by me one day, irritates me the next. I don't want a stranger sitting at my table right now.

I like being touched. I'm a hugger. In most photographs I'm leaning into a friend and they have their arm around me.

I don't like sharing my space. *"Can we meet at your place?"* makes me feel trapped. I don't want to say no. It feels cutting and rude. But it feels worse to find myself with someone in my apartment.

I believe in generosity. I will go out of my way to put others before myself. This makes me feel expansive and in control. A lot of my happiness resides in my ability to do things for others.

If anger creeps in, or resentment, I have overstepped. I have neglected myself, and that is a boundary I will defend and be unwilling to negotiate.

No one else can do this for me.

Obstacles To Writing

It's really hard to make a living as a writer.

It takes up a lot of time too.

Time I can't spend with anyone but myself.

And, to clear my mind, I tend to want to get everything else done first.

If I want to write I have to do it a lot. Writing is a muscle that needs regular exercise. If I skip a day or two I feel the darn thing beginning to ossify.

I have to put it first because what I leave for last never gets done.

What you leave for last will not get done.

Paradoxically, I have to feed it. If all I do is sit and write I have no input and will run out of new things to say.

I have to open my mind and consider my life to be an offering.

I write no matter what. I don't care about the money or your approval or if you want to recognize me or give me an award.

I mean, I care. But I'm not going to dwell on any of these things because I need that juice to write.

The obstacles to writing are the same things stopping anyone from doing anything that serves no purpose other than to feed the soul.

An Option

It is my perception that suicidal thoughts are typically regarded as a symptom on the extreme side of depression.

Except I have often contemplated suicide without even feeling particularly depressed.

For me, suicide is always an option, and considering it a form of escape. *"This is not a bad day to die. I wouldn't have to go to that meeting that I'm dreading."*

Once, a long time ago, I mentioned this to my (then) husband. *"Suicide is a viable alternative. A choice, ever available to us."*

He looked at me utterly stunned.

"Dushka, no. I have never, ever considered killing myself an option."

Huh.

Through the years the subject of suicide has come up in conversation with close friends. My extremely empirical research indicates that the thought never occurs to some people, even when they are depressed; and is ever available to others, even when they are not.

Here I want to add that there is something about breakups that I always found particularly devastating. A bad one would unglue me, in a way that other experiences of loss did not (I don't mean one hurt more or less—just that the damage was different).

After a bad breakup the option to die rather than feel how I felt was quite attractive.

I opened my eyes in the morning and before getting up had to decide if I would live.

I have a close, loving friend who is a therapist. I tried talking to her once. She said *"I have to ask you, for ethical reasons, if you think you could be a danger to yourself."*

"I just told you I want to kill myself," I replied. *"Of course I'm a danger to myself."*

Getting older has shifted things. It has either made me stronger or granted me the perspective to take breakups and other painful incidents more in stride.

I did learn that it takes a bad moment for someone to resolve to die. Not a bad life. Not even a bad week. Just a moment that aligns in such a way that the whole world points to only one logical conclusion.

I know that postponing that decision even a few hours alters the perspective of how much sense suicide seems to make, how from one second to the other it becomes the only answer.

I know too that it is not a "selfish" decision. Really what you want is to not be a burden, and to not have to carry the unbearable weight that life suddenly becomes.

"Happy" is one of my defining characteristics. I am sunny, an optimist. Without exerting much effort I see the bright side of everything.

I love life so much it makes me feel my chest will burst.

Perhaps in equal proportion I have the capacity, however temporary, to feel its sharp edges and its darkness.

I Don't Know What I Want

I went to the supermarket this morning. I was really hungry.

What do I want for breakfast? Salty? Sweet?

Something light and quick or something filling?

Eggs and toast, maybe with an avocado sliced on top? Bean tacos? A cup of coffee and a hearty cookie? A muffin? Maybe chai and fruit!

I really, really want something, but I don't know what.

A woman is standing in front of me drinking a chocolate protein drink. I ask her if it's good.

"It's the most delicious protein shake I've ever had," she says.

I grab one, open it and take a big slug. As a food lover, I never would have thought *"I want a protein shake"* but it's creamy and thick and satisfying and I feel like my whole body is thanking me for choosing just what I needed.

This is what life is like.

I don't know what I want.

Instead of feeling angst about this, which makes me feel inadequate, nervous, fearful, stressed, closed off, I have learned that not knowing what I want is a gift, not a curse.

It keeps me receptive, open and ready to welcome the perfect thing.

The Cure For Pain

The last time I went through a devastating breakup many well intentioned people offered me advice.

After such a long, monogamous relationship what you need to shake things up is to sleep around.

Jump back into another relationship right away! A nail removes another!

I know you don't drink/do drugs but it would really help you relax.

Take a trip! Get away from it all!

I did indeed travel, and found I had efficiently packed all my pain in the roomy suitcase that is my chest.

I regret to inform you there is no getting away from pain.

What I ended up doing was sitting with it. I spent sleepless nights hugging my knees and crying. I cried a river; maybe an ocean.

Being heartbroken is terrifying. Breakups have a particular way of scraping out my insides.

This "sitting with pain" doesn't feel good, but it's so much more effective than running or distracting myself from it. These two things leave me feeling empty and depressed.

In my experience, the more I run, the more it's there.

Once I let it hit me and come out on the other side I am less afraid.

If I can get through that I can get through anything.

And that's why Rumi says the cure for pain is in the pain.

Cost Of Admission

Regret is like poison and antidote rolled into a single word.

It's really hard to learn anything if you don't royally mess things up.

I have done things—hurtful things, careless things, stupid things—that I fervently wish I had done differently.

But, if I hadn't done that, I wouldn't be the person I am today.

And, I wouldn't be on my way to becoming the person I will become.

It's not so much that I don't have regret.

It's that I regard regret as the cost of admission to compassion, to maturity, to happiness.

The Good People

One day at a party I was sitting on one side of a long couch with Boyfriend. I had my hand resting on his leg and we were talking.

From the other side of the couch a woman leans over. *"Hey, Dushka's Boyfriend!"* she coos. *"I haven't seen you in so long! You look great! Tell me, why are you sitting all the way over there, when I'm all the way over here?"*

Jealousy is one of my inner dragons. I used to suffer from it immensely, and through a lot of work I have effectively reduced it to the point of feeling my view of the world and the way I see relationships has been forever altered.

But this was sudden. Where I come from, jealousy is required to "take care of your man."

I definitely wouldn't want to be careless.

I turn to this woman and have a clear mental image of me flying over the couch in slow motion and pouncing on top of her.

Instead I sit there frozen with a smile plastered on my face.

"Boyfriend has a past," I tell myself. "*He met many women before he met you, just like you met many men before meeting him. It is incredibly selfish for you to take this like a personal affront.*

"Pull yourself together."

I sit there poised like a queen drinking high tea. The woman sashays over. Boyfriend introduces us. I say hello and we resume our conversation.

The only person who notices anything out of the ordinary is annoyingly perceptive Boyfriend, who claims my left eyebrow twitched.

I'm a good person.

But because I am human the good in me comes mixed with other things, like a frothy cocktail in my soul of doubt, apathy, self-centeredness and ignorance.

Whenever I detect something in another that I don't like, that's how I know that I carry it in myself.

It's a foolproof way of telling what I need to work on.

An Enjoyable Thing

I am very neat.

This is more a compulsion than a virtue. I don't strive for order. It's not that I'm disciplined or that I have a system. It's that I am uncomfortable living any other way.

The busier I am, the more I need to line things up (and I don't mean metaphorically). In a world of people who tend to shop when they need a boost, I tend to de-clutter for an equivalent fix of relief.

My inbox is always clean. As I read my email, I delete whatever does not require action. I seldom file things. I throw out whatever I suspect I won't remember that I have (To me, if you don't remember owning it, that is equal to not having it).

My desk looks like no one works there because any stack of paper would be to me like a poke in the eye would be to you.

My house doesn't have anything in it that I don't find either useful or beautiful. I keep in my closet empty shopping bags, where I toss something the minute I realize I'm not going to wear it.

I feel that considering that a thing has sentimental value is somewhat of an oxymoron. I have a friend who correctly accused me of having a *"Hyper-Zen drive to divest myself of all material possessions."*

If Boyfriend has a pile of something around the house (socks, papers, magazines), I explain to him that I feel as if it were piled on my chest. It's not that I'm being tidy. It's that I need to not suffocate.

Creating order out of chaos is not something I'd ever consider a chore. It clears my head. I do it for fun. Doing laundry is instant gratification. Taking something rumpled, stained and smelly and turning it into something fresh, fluffy and neatly stacked is my idea of heaven.

Please don't be like me. We each need to pursue whatever makes our life a pleasure to live it. If you are messy, embrace it. Disorganization can be healthy. I've read that *"the costs of maintaining order are often overlooked. That time could be spent doing more enjoyable things."*

Go do your own definition of "an enjoyable thing" while I go arrange Boyfriend's spice rack in alphabetical order.

My Puppy Heart

I kissed a boy once. I thought I loved him and found out a day later he kissed me on a dare.

I would never let how he hurt me close me off to love but I did become more purposeful, less careless, about who I gave my heart to. My puppy heart, always so eager and happy to love.

Some time later another boy told me he wanted to go steady with me, back when that meant pointing at someone from afar and claiming *"That's my girlfriend."* I consented.

Another boy asked me the same question and I said yes to him too. I did not realize their feelings would be hurt.

I learned to be careful, so careful with the fragile, sacred heart of those who chose to love me.

I learned too to keep an eye on my vanity. Another person was more important than feeling wanted. It had to be. I have tried to keep her in check ever since.

You don't toy with someone's feelings just so you can feel better about yourself.

There was this other boy. He didn't love me back but I spent a lot of time daydreaming about what it would be like if he did.

After a few weeks of expending a lot of energy in this daydreaming I realized I could not let myself get lost in someone else like that.

I understood all of this before I turned sixteen but have had to learn it again and again.

Don't Chase The Pain

I have a friend who is a physical therapist.

After years of doing this work he tells me he has learned *"it never works to chase the pain."*

He has to instead look for *"what is taking the train off the tracks."*

Say a patient comes in and claims his knee hurts. My friend doesn't automatically look at the knee or look to treat the knee.

Knee pain could be an ankle injury or a hip injury or a pulled muscle.

Knee pain is not always related to the knee.

If something is making me suffer for a reason that seems trite or I have a recurring struggle or fight, I remind myself not to chase the pain.

What is the larger issue?

What is this really about?

What is it that is taking the train off the tracks?

That is the place I need to work on.

I Command Me

Sleep is a very important part of being healthy and I don't sleep very well.

I try to go to bed early but often wake up in the middle of the night and want to bounce out of bed to get something done.

I attempt to convince myself to stay where I am and calm down and go back to sleep.

Come on. Deep breaths. Nothing needs to get done right this minute.

Please, please just this one thing and then we will be free.

Dushka. If you get up you will walk around and turn the light on and go to the computer and then you're done. You won't come back to bed.

Yes I will, I will just this quick thing IT IS IMPORTANT WE ARE SO IMPORTANT WE DON'T HAVE TIME TO SLEEP.

So many contradicting thoughts all in the same brain.

But, I don't need to listen to all my thoughts.

I don't need to react to everything I think.

Some thoughts I can just look at and distance myself from.

Oh, look! There is a thought, suggesting I get out of bed. Interesting. I guess I'm agitated. But we're all staying right here. We need our rest.

We are all going to settle down.

Under that big tangle of thoughts is me.

I am command and control.

I respectfully regard all the thoughts. I listen and notice and nod and give them all their place.

I hear you want to get up. I know you believe there is a crisis to solve. Thank you for bringing that to my attention! But we're OK. It can wait until morning.

It's My Name

In Mexico, where I'm from, a woman is expected to take her husband's last name.

By "expected" I mean it's almost like it's not even a choice.

I love my name. It's what I use to identify myself.

Hello, I'm Dushka Zapata.

Giving it up seemed so strange. It felt like I would erase a part of me.

I couldn't do it.

So, I didn't.

If I got married again it would be even harder for me to change my name.

"Zapata" is my father's last name and he died recently. I carry him with me always, every time I introduce myself or sign something.

Of course I would carry him with me anyway, but why give up something that makes me feel like he's keeping me company?

This decision is intensely personal. Changing your name to someone else's can be symbolic and a beautiful way to begin a new life with someone else.

It's just not for me.

To Improve Your Vocabulary

I think in words. To quote Wittgenstein, *"The limits of my language are the limits of my mind. I don't know what I don't have words for."*

When I write, I do so with a dictionary and a thesaurus within reach. This way, if I want to tell you about an unease I can't quite describe that is more discreet than distress I know I can call it apprehension or disquiet.

When I read, I look up words even when I think I can infer their meaning from how they look or sound. Because vexillology is not the science of annoying or irritating things.

I listen to the radio, watch TV and listen to books on tape. I talk to people who have different areas of expertise. I notice etymology, hoping for clues (when Theseus went into the infamous labyrinth he unraveled a "clew", a ball of string his lover gave him, to find his way back out).

I collect words that cannot be translated into other languages, like *sobremesa* (the time you spend at the table chatting after you are done eating) or *kummerspeck* (the weight you gain when you eat because you are sad. It literally translates into grief bacon.).

To expand your vocabulary, read. Write. Look up words in the dictionary. Flip through the dictionary for fun. But mostly, love words. Love them with fervor, with ardor, with vigor, with lust. Love them into the opposite of oblivion.

Crush

I am extremely prone to frequent crushes.

Back when I felt that developing intense feelings for someone merited a reaction from the object of my crush, I found this emotional tangle terribly painful.

Until I learned that they had nothing to do with anyone but me and that they were a gift.

A crush is a pure lightning bolt of the best kind of energy. It's mine to use any way I see fit.

I use it to wake up happy and create something.

To fuel the courage to do less of what depletes me and more of what fulfills me.

To love myself for exactly who I am.

To use it as motivation to always be kind, even after a long day.

Years from now, when I look back at the time I had a crush on a stranger, rather than thinking *"Boy, that was so silly!"* I remember what I felt as a source of inspiration.

Inspiration is what a crush is for.

The Most Powerful Tool

Practice is revolutionary.

It is the most underestimated, most powerful tool available to us.

It's the door to understanding something. To learning something. To getting good at something. To getting better at something.

It's the way to accomplish something I never thought I could.

It's how something I previously thought impossible one day becomes easy.

Let's say I want to become a good writer. What will it take?

Practice. To be a good writer, I need to write.

Let's say I'm going to practice from Monday to Sunday, every day.

If I start on Monday, will I be slightly better by Friday?

Not necessarily.

Monday might be rusty. Tuesday might be smoother. Wednesday, catastrophic. Thursday I want to give up and never practice again.

This isn't working. Why did I think this was a good idea?

Friday is frustrating and difficult.

Saturday is smooth.

Sunday is—

What a waste.

The lesson here is not in getting better or worse but in how I meet my bad days and my good days.

Do I get exasperated? Do I give up? Do I run?

I want to run.

Can I learn to meet my bad days with equanimity, to have bad days not matter so that my emotions remain stable while my skill does what it will?

Practice cannot be about right or wrong.

It's a gift: something I can count on forever.

It will always be there waiting for me.

Even if I get everything wrong a thousand times I can always, always begin again.

Being Single

When I am single here is the advice I give myself: learn how to be happy now. Right now with what you have and what you don't, whatever that is.

Waiting for anything outside of me to make me happy—for tomorrow to come, for the project to end, for another job, the right man, when my haircut grows out, when I lose a pound, when Friday rolls around—means I will always be waiting for something.

Things I've Thrown Out

The notion that there is a mysterious, enigmatic element to insomnia. Instead, I work towards sleeping better.

The concept of dieting. No diet works.

The belief that I need to or even could win someone's love.

Any voice, inside or out that in any way suggests I am not enough. In that same swoop I threw out the fear that I would one day not have enough. I will always have enough and if one day I don't I trust that I will be able to figure it out.

Comparing myself to anyone. Besides, surrounding myself with people who are better than me is a glorious way to live.

The assumption that I don't deserve to have wonderful things happen to me, one after the other, in absurd excess. The other shoe is not going to drop. There is no limit to how happy I can be, and the same thing goes for you.

"Some Day" Will Never Be Today

I always knew I'd write a book.

I expected it to happen a lot sooner and it didn't.

The absence of the book disappointed me. (*What? These things don't just materialize on their own?*)

Whenever I ran into someone I had not seen for years (thank you, Facebook!) *"Where's your book?"* was the first question they asked.

The nerve.

I don't have an answer to why it took me so long.

No, wait. Yes I do.

I traveled and moved countries and got married and worked a lot and got myself a career and I expected the book would appear some day and some day never became today.

One day I woke up to the fact that "some day" would not come until I called it "right now".

This awakening only took about three decades.

I took stock of what I had already written and decided that it deserved being assembled all in one place.

Not scattered into different notebooks or in the form of very short stories I was posting across social media channels.

I needed, today, to stop kidding around and get cracking on a book series.

A collection.

The first time I saw my book in book form—the cover and the contents all assembled into a single place—I anticipated a sense of accomplishment.

What I actually felt knocked the wind out of me.

I felt terror.

I was nervous and scared and felt like my book and my effort was worthless.

I briefly entertained throwing it all out and aborting the mission but I published it anyway.

That same night I came down with a flu. I was in bed with a fever for over a week.

This startling fear and nerves and sense of absolute worthlessness (*I need to throw this out! It's shit! Total shit!*) of course propelled me into immediately writing my second book, and my third.

Creating something that lays you out like that is ghastly.

I vigorously recommend that you do it.

It doesn't have to be a book.

It's whatever opens up your insides and offers them to the world.

Struggle

When I am in yoga class and trying to get into an advanced pose I struggle to tell the difference between pushing myself and taking care of myself.

I don't think I can do that but I'm going to try.

Am I being brave? Or am I letting my ego get in the way and trying too hard and risking injury?

I'm not going to try.

Am I being prudent and responsible or not trying hard enough and being complacent or lazy?

Where is my edge?

This struggle to distinguish one from the other holds true across all areas of my life.

Counterintuitive Life Lessons

You think you know what you want, but you don't.

Making a choice means rejecting everything else. If you believe you know what you want you begin turning things down before giving them a chance.

Who you are somewhere is who you are everywhere.

If you learn something somewhere, you learn it everywhere.

You are not supposed to avoid pain.

Pain is your body's way of saying "don't try this again". It works to keep you safe (once you try touching an open flame you know not to try that again) but in other aspects of life getting hurt is the only way to learn something.

Don't touch an open flame but definitely fall in love. You'll get hurt for sure, but who wants to live without that?

The term "self-fulfilling prophecy" is really a thing.

I suffer from insomnia and am sometimes so stressed about not getting enough sleep that the stress keeps me awake. So, if you can make bad things come true, you have equal power to make good things come true.

Deriving joy from being alone is required to being in good company.

Learning to rejoice in your own company is the only way to attract healthy relationships.

More often than not you need to do less rather than more.

Getting enough sleep, being idle, spending time relaxing, giving yourself a day with nothing specific to do, are all the key to looking at things differently and fostering creativity.

Trying to get everything perfect is a flaw and does not lead to success.

A perfectionist is driven by insecurity. Ambition is driven by hunger.

Too many goals are not the key to accomplishment.

Too many goals leave no room for all the surprises life has in store for you that you can't possibly plan for. This is called serendipity, and it's a fragile, beautiful thing that needs space and free time.

Disappointing people is essential to a happy life.

I don't want to disappoint anyone who loves me. But it's the only way to make your life your own.

You are less vulnerable if you tell people who you really are.

Your secrets matter less than you think, and chances are high people already know.

Resentment

When I feel resentment it's because someone asked something of me that I didn't want to do and I did it anyway.

In other words, my boundaries weren't clear—to myself.

This means (to me) that feeling resentment towards someone else is misplaced resentment, when really I feel it towards myself.

The clearer I am on my boundaries and the clearer I articulate them to others, the less resentment I feel.

Sometimes it's necessary to say no and doing so is my responsibility.

This realization helps me take this responsibility off the shoulders of another person.

Repetition

I stumble along, clumsy and eager, crashing against things that make me suffer.

I think a lot about this suffering, turn it around in my head to try to find where it's really coming from and how I can put my perspective in a place where things will hurt me less.

Sometimes I find a logic that works and write about it so I don't forget it.

It's not "advice", you see. It's an offering of something that worked for me that others might find useful. Or not.

Despite all these notes I forget anyway, stumble along, clumsy and eager, crash against something I already know will make me suffer and find myself having to learn the lesson again and again.

Life is not a collection of peaks and pinnacles and adventures.

Life is repetition.

This repetition, this inevitable relearning of the same lessons, is where you can find the most reliable kind of joy.

There is solace in persistence, in knowing that despite my mistakes and my flaws I can always begin again.

I'm stubborn, and distracted, and forgetful, and careless, so I frequently ignore all these notes I took to help my future self.

But I always find refuge in daily acts of the most ordinary kind of devotion, in writing and the flower that sits on my desk.

This to me defines both happiness and success. I experience both again and again and again.

The Virtue In Indecision

I am very decisive. My brain believes that making a decision—any decision, even the wrong one—is better than making no decision at all.

Being decisive means closing yourself off to everything except what you decide.

Being indecisive means all options remain open.

I lose sight of the fact that confusion can be a privileged, exalted state.

Remaining in this state often allows me to find a path through many obstacles and challenges.

Fact: Living in uncertainty creates opportunity.

Sometimes, I don't need to decide. Sometimes I need to wait. Remind me.

Detachment

I wanted so badly to remain detached.

Until I realized that wanting badly to remain detached was me being attached to detachment.

What if rather than feeling perpetually torn between a spiritual life and a practical one I could use one to teach me about the other?

What if my entire life was meant to be a practice?

Can I keep a quiet mind and an even breath in insane traffic?

Can I remain fully in the present when I'm stressed about tomorrow's meeting?

Can I set my ego aside when ferociously fighting with Boyfriend?

I might not be able to move to a temple in Japan any time soon, but here are some places where I can practice non attachment right here, right now:

Getting my ego out of the way. (This alone will keep me fully occupied forever.)

Identifying and removing the stories I tell myself about the world and others.

How can I come from a place of love regardless of the circumstances?

How can I make sure I always have time to listen to myself?

How can I diminish resentment?

How can I not let fear be my guide?

How can I be aware of my attachments? (You can't mend what you can't see.)

How can I let go of patterns in my behavior?

How can I be more conscious of the consequences of my every action?

How can I stop blaming others?

How can I always tell the truth, even to myself?

How can I stop wanting what I don't need?

How can I need less?

All of these things are exercises that move me towards a life of non-attachment while making it possible for me to remain fully in my reality.

I have a family and friends and a roof over my head and I am unwilling to let that go.

Fortunately, I have a lot of work to do before I even get to that point.

Happiness Is Elusive

Every so often I am overwhelmed by a feeling of well being.

And then I wonder if "well being" does a good job describing it.

It's not a rush, like joy or enthusiasm (which fortunately I'm also prone to). It's softer and fuller. Should I call it "Wellness"? Nah. Too clinical. This is more akin to fulfillment, to (dare I say it?) happiness.

Maybe it just needs a bit of Italian flair. *Benessere.*

Or, Greek. *Eudaimonia.*

The point is that, regrettably, I've come to discover that it's not a feeling I can chase. It has to come on its own. I can't find it in good meals, in conversations with friends or the company of people I love. It's not in a spa, even if the massage was a particularly good one. It doesn't present itself when I buy new shoes, or finalize a good document. It doesn't hold hands with the (delightful) sense of a job well done. It's unpredictable. It always surprises me.

It shows up quietly, say, when I travel and am surrounded by unfamiliar sights, smells, sounds. But it doesn't come on every trip.

It arrives when I'm sitting somewhere, not making an effort to do three things at once. When I'm just taking the world in.

But if I tell myself to focus on staying in the present and just enjoying the moment for what it is, it evades me.

Is this what happiness is? An elusive, ephemeral tease of a feeling that you can't consciously go after?

It might be my inalienable right to pursue it, but if I do, I might miss it entirely.

Your Constant Reminder

After my last break up I realized the importance of the place where I live.

I wake up in it and come home to it and, as such, it has a huge impact on how I perceive the world.

Despite my frugal nature, I went out searching for the very best apartment I could possibly afford to rent. Spacious, quiet, sunny, safe.

I wanted to open my eyes in the morning and not feel punished for my decision.

The place where I was living stood as my constant reminder that I could look out for myself and that everything was going to be OK.

Looking back on this I feel it was the very best thing I could have done for myself.

How To Suffer Less

My Dad died a year ago. In this year I have given a lot of thought to how *painful* losing him was, but also how much I *suffered* more than I needed to due to the anticipation of pain, fear and the stories I told myself.

When he first told me he had cancer what I felt was terror. This terror was due mostly to the fact that I assumed he would be in agonizing physical pain.

I was extremely distressed at not being a good enough daughter. Would I be able to be there for him every time he needed me to be despite the fact my whole life was in another country?

I had a lot of anxiety around the relationship with all his children (my siblings). Would we stand strong, support each other? What if this tore us apart?

I had a lot of concerns around the financial implications of this disease: the cost of surgeries, treatment, medical care.

While there were a lot of things we would all have to face that I never anticipated, a lot of what I suffered over never happened.

Although I had my share of bad days, in a general sense as he got sicker I made an effort to only feel *pain* in relation to what was immediately before me.

I believe this is what got me through the loss of a parent. Setting aside all the *suffering* around things that were not real —not immediately, in the present moment real—and dealing only with right now.

In this sense we can be more responsible—or, to put it in other words—have more control over our suffering. A lot of what causes us to suffer is a figment of our imagination.

We do not have the stamina to handle things that have not taken place.

Plaits And Spirals

The last time I muttered to myself I was having "a bad day" I noted all the little things that were going my way that in my funk I might not have seen.

My bus, which tends to be late, showed up right when I did. A stranger's kid came over to say hello.

I ordered a salad and it had pomegranate seeds in it. They looked like misplaced jewelry in a bowl of green.

I decided I needed to go home and lie down and took a deep, satisfying nap I woke up groggy from. I found lemonade in the refrigerator.

I prefer to reject the notion of "a bad day". It forces me to apply too broad a label throwing out the good with the bad, missing out on life's daily ordinary offerings.

You overlook the sweet, unexpected beauty within bad things.

You fail to see strange, twined gifts to be grateful for, the plaits and spirals that are in everything.

Restlessness

I miss Boyfriend. I want to hear his voice. I really shouldn't be calling him at work, but it will be just one quick hello and then I won't miss him so much.

I have a long to-do list. I check something off the to-do list and it makes me feel a sense of accomplishment. (Sometimes, I write things on the to-do list that I have already done, just to give myself the pleasure of checking them off.)

I tell myself that I will only have one more chocolate covered blueberry. One more, and then I will be done.

When I'm meditating, I am sitting really, really still and begin to feel uncomfortable. My ankle hurts and my forehead itches. If I move just a little bit, scratch a little bit, I will be comfortable and then I will really be able to focus on my breath.

Now here is the truth:

Calling Boyfriend and saying hello does not make me feel like I miss him less. Calling him makes me feel like I interrupted him, like I shouldn't have, and like I still miss him. Now I want to call him to tell him I am sorry I interrupted him.

My to-do list is long. It will always be long. Checking things off gives me a tiny, quick hit of satisfaction followed by an immediate *"I am so very busy"* feeling, followed by adding three more things I need to get done. My quick and dirty sense of accomplishment is gone. Now I want to be busier.

I don't have to tell you how the *"one more chocolate covered berry"* story goes. Just give me the bag.

When I meditate and sit very still and decide to move then I just want to move more. Moving my ankle is followed by a chain of adjusting and scratching that brings no relief at all.

I need to sit with my feelings. Rather than address them or satiate them or give myself any immediate gratification or do anything about them, I need to just sit.

Eventually I am reminded that I don't need to call anyone or be busier or eat more or wiggle.

I don't need anything at all.

Introverts And Parties

I wish I loved parties. I'd see my friends more often and we'd laugh and chat and toast with sparkling, bubbly drinks served in long stemmed festive fluted glasses.

I'd go to bars and sip fruity tropical cocktails that would leave my lips covered in salt and sugar from the glass rims.

I'd kiss strangers with those lips and they would taste like rum.

I would go to discotheques and sway to loud booming music until dawn.

I'd spend the next day recovering from the night instead of getting up early.

I realize that wishing for all these things is really me wishing for easy happiness.

It's me somewhere at some point having bought into the illusion that these things would bring me a kind of instant joy.

It's me convinced I am somehow inadequate for not being interested in any of this.

But I'm not.

I mean, I might be inadequate, but I'm not interested.

Even writing about wishing for these things feels unnatural, like I'm betraying myself.

I sometimes wish I liked these things but stronger than that wish is me really liking that I don't.

I dig who I am. I like the relief and utter freedom I feel when I walk out of a noisy place and set myself right every step I take away from it.

I like that I have friends I adore who love these things and who completely understand I just want to go home.

The best kind of happiness is ferocious because you fight for it, you stand up for it and you reclaim it over and over.

The reward is that you have yourself to return to.

Sanskara

Do you know what a sanskara is?

Let's say that when I am 16 I have a boyfriend and he cheats on me, causing me great pain. This pain leaves an imprint. I really don't want to go through this pain again, so my insides associate "boyfriend" with "cheating".

One day I meet a man who has no intention of cheating on me. I regard him with suspicion and am unable to trust him because of my sanskara.

We all have sanskaras, and everything that happens to us is stored in the form of a memory initially intended to protect us. *(Be careful with men! That hurt a lot!)*

Our work is to become aware of our sanskaras so we can distinguish between our personal imprints and the true nature of the people before us.

Sanskaras are extremely difficult to change as they are rooted deep inside us.

More importantly, you can't change what you cannot see.

I believe that a relationship with someone very different from you can make many of your sanskaras evident, visible. They make you aware.

This awareness comes with an enormous gift: the opportunity to decide what is more important to you: holding on to your sanskara, or your relationship.

Brutal Honesty

Have you ever noticed how often we lie?

I don't mean an malicious intent to deceive (although, that too).

I mean the insidious lies we tell to avoid hurting someone's feelings, to weasel out of uncomfortable situations, to satisfy the insatiable beast that is social protocol.

I'm telling you, we lie constantly.

Here is an example: I am an introvert.

I can't even tell you the amount of excuses I used to make to avoid attending parties or get-togethers without hurting people's feelings. *"I am so busy at work." "I have a previous commitment." "Regrettably, I will be traveling."*

Or worse. I can't tell you the amount of times I attended things I didn't want to attend and ended up exhausted, resentful, angry.

One day, it hit me: even when loving and well intentioned, lies erode my life. They erode my relationships. They make me be less of who I am.

As they add up, they make me lose my way.

So now I make an effort to tell the truth.

I don't think telling the truth requires it to be brutal, though.

I try to tell the truth kindly, tactfully, but unequivocally.

"I can't attend your party," I say. *"I need to go home and look out the window."*

Resolving to tell the truth has changed my life. My friends accept me for who I am. The work I do is a better fit to my interests and expertise. My time is spent in places that matter to me.

Added bonus: telling the truth becomes easier and easier.

Laundry Zen

I just completed a basic training to become a yoga teacher. One of the most interesting things I learned is that true skill does not lie in my ability (or lack thereof) to wrap my leg behind my neck, but rather in being interested in the layers of complexity found in even the most simple poses.

I have tried to apply this lesson to my daily life, recognizing the meditative quality in neatly, perfectly folding still-warm clothes, the intricacy in sorting a large pile of only slightly dissimilar looking socks, welcoming the rhythm and efficiency in cleaning dishes and cups.

There is enormous detail in the most simple things; just like very complex things can be made simple.

It's up to me to find what I am looking for.

Your Regard For Yourself

Self-esteem is how you regard yourself.

It affects everything because it is what you see the world through.

It manifests in how you treat yourself and how you teach others to treat you.

Some symptoms of healthy self-esteem:

The understanding that you are worthy of love right now.

Not when you become a morning person, when you lose weight, or when you get around to cleaning out your garage.

You can't guarantee someone loves you, but you know you are lovable, and that is enough.

You take care for yourself.

You are willing to take a risk that involves overcoming fear (such as asking someone out on a date) but you don't engage in risky behavior that could hurt you (such as getting in the car when you know the person driving has had too much to drink).

Your regard for yourself is inside, not outside.

Approval is delicious, but it doesn't define you. And, while you listen carefully to others, ultimately you know you need to listen to yourself.

Your boundaries are clear:

I am sorry if what I do disappoints you, but you don't get to force me into doing what you think is best for me.

You don't take things personally.

Chances are high that it's not about you.

You are not threatened by your own fallibility.

You respect another's opinion even if it's different from your own, you acknowledge your mistakes and are comfortable saying you are sorry.

Throughout your life your degree of self-esteem tends to ebb and flow.

A healthy self-esteem requires both practice and awareness and is built by your perspective and the choices that you make.

Self-esteem is not something that you have or that you lose. It's something that you work at, and you can always begin again.

An Alternative

We live in a culture obsessed with being "The Best".

If by definition, only one can be "The Best", where does that leave everyone else?

Resentful, that's where. Not just unfulfilled: unfillable. Not just unsatisfied: insatiable. If this is the case, if most people feel like losers most of the time, then there is a fatal flaw in the initial proposition.

Why, then, are we buying into it?

What if, instead, we focused on Being? Not The Best. Just Being.

Maybe:

We'd stop running, chasing, clutching. We're not lost. We're here.

We'd listen. Not look at the person who's talking while our minds are vagrant. Not nodding while sneaking peaks at our cell phones. We'd stop. And listen.

We'd exercise, every day, an earnest effort to put someone else's needs before our own.

We'd love with abandon. Not through the land mines of our insecurities.

We'd realize that what we do to ourselves has indelible consequences that will catch up with us.

We wouldn't wonder what it all means, if this is all there is, or what we're supposed to do next.

We would be defined by what we are, not by what we do.

We'd be left, in the end, with something more valuable than perfection.

Perfection is overrated.

Arm Balances

When I started doing yoga I would look at what everyone else could do and tell myself I would never get there.

Some poses, in particular arm balances, defy gravity.

Instead of thinking of all the things I couldn't do, instead of wondering when I could possibly accomplish all of them (which often leads to getting discouraged) I decided I would show up as often as I could to class, breathe, and move through the poses.

Today. I will do the best I can today.

That's how I surprised myself by getting into poses I never thought I could. By doing my best right now. By showing up as often as possible. By respecting where I was at on that day.

Show up. Practice. Breathe. Don't look at what others are doing. Push yourself. Take care of yourself. Repeat.

This is not only the recipe for a successful arm balance.

It's the recipe for everything.

After A Break Up

I tie a lot of who I am to my relationships.

My relationship with my significant other is very important to me and I have a tendency to dissolve "me" into "we".

The experience of breaking up has always been painful, terrifying and incredibly good for me as it serves to remind myself who I am, what is important to me, what I like, and how I want to spend my life.

After a break up I take stock of everything. I ask myself a lot of questions. Am I doing what I love? Am I spending my time in the right places? What are all these things coming up and how did I not see them?

Was this me, or me trying to be what another person wanted me to be or thought I was? What can I learn from this? How can I be a better person?

A lot of change tends to follow, mostly liberating, wonderful change. Not only big, sweeping things. A new haircut. A change in style (who was the person who used to wear all these clothes?), a reassessment of my life.

The change, while tumultuous, has always left me in a better place.

I like to think that after decades of this I have gotten better. I have learned to love myself and to keep a strong identity even within a relationship. It's difficult, and a balancing act.

I am a work in progress.

If I felt I was on the wrong course I would take a step back and take a good, close look at everything.

The journey to who I am—which switches, starts over, and course corrects frequently—is, in my opinion, what life is all about.

Relish it. Make it an adventure.

How To Be Less Boring

Boring is a relative term. How it's defined depends on who you ask.

I don't like big parties. I don't like to stay up late (unless I'm writing). I don't like small talk so when someone chit chats I don't know what to say.

I have an aversion to noise (I startle easily).

I don't drink and don't do drugs.

For a long time—in particular when I was growing up—I was sure there was something wrong with me. Not being invited to a party made me feel left out. Being invited made me angsty.

When I was out, all I wanted to do was return home. Parties bore me, but they also make me feel isolated.

As you can see, I was not much fun.

Then something changed. I liked who I was.

I realized the problem was trying to conform to another's definition of "fun" instead of my own.

I decide what is boring.

Being "interesting" or "boring" is personal.

To be less boring, be less boring to yourself.

Midlife Crisis

When I hear the term "midlife crisis" the first thing I think about is a fancy red car and a very young lover.

But that is not what it means to me.

To me, it means waking up one day to realizations that look like this:

How did I end up here?

I need to start over.

How is it that I have everything I want and I'm still not happy?

This can't be all there is. Can it?

As a result of these realizations you begin to make changes, sometimes drastic, sometimes desperate, not always wise, in an effort to put yourself in a better position.

Because this is your life, and you only have one, and you are running out of time.

Which gives rise to another beautiful question.

If not now, when?

These efforts are usually met by aggressive disapproval, because no one likes change and the people who love you want you to remain the person they know.

This reinforces what you have been feeling: that no one else will live your life for you and that therefore there is only one authority on the matter: you.

So off you go, experimenting, exploring, stumbling.

Less comfortable for sure, but so much more *alive.*

This makes you re-evaluate your definition of happiness.

It's not about stuff but about being awake.

What you want is for your life to mean something.

For me, a midlife crisis is coming into your own power.

It's what I wish upon everyone.

The Most Beautiful Thing

A lie, even a tempting one, even a so-called "merciful" one, even a so-called "necessary" one, even one you tell yourself, hurts like shrapnel.

It tears into you, jagged, messy, leaves debris behind.

It will take a long time to identify just how much damage it has done.

More often than not a lie requires another. The new one wraps around the old like a grimy bandage.

Initially it feels tight and safe but underneath rampant infection is inevitable.

You will have to cut out a lot in an attempt to get things back to the way they were, but they never do.

Years later you are still removing shards of metal from the wound.

The truth instead comes in precise, like a cut inflicted with an expensive Japanese knife. Of course it hurts, but it slices clean. It will burn, bleed—maybe profusely—but it will heal quickly and leave the smallest of scars.

Truth, sharp and raw and lethal.

Truth is the most beautiful thing.

Male For A Day

I once saw a documentary (if I could remember the name, I would reference it) of a slender woman who wears a costume that makes her look morbidly obese.

She wears this costume for a week experiencing first hand how morbidly obese people are treated.

The insight breaks her heart. It changes her life.

I saw another documentary (unrelated to the first one, and I cannot remember the name of this one either) of a man who wears a suit designed to make him feel as if he was very old.

The costume is heavy and allows for diminished movement in his joints.

A flight of stairs he normally would not have noticed becomes an obstacle almost too big to handle.

He understands what it means to be terrified of having to go downstairs.

I have always been curious about what it would be like to walk in someone else's shoes (or in the case of this question, in someone else's body).

I think such experiences would make us all better people.

What would it be like to be a man?

Would I offer to be the one to take the gigantic spider outside? Would I be able to easily open that jar? Would I be horrified if I suddenly felt like sobbing? Would I feel a need to spread out in order to occupy more space than strictly necessary? Would I require larger servings of food?

Would I be less concerned about walking back from my bus stop in the dark?

What kind of pressure or fear or obligation would I be under that today, as a woman, I cannot fathom?

What is it that you struggle with that doesn't even occur to us to talk about?

I would love the chance to be male for one day. I would understand you guys better and be even more grateful for all the things you do for us.

The Meaning Of Words

What does "home made" mean?

When you bring a pie to someone's house and say it's "home made" should it be inferred that you made it in your kitchen?

And, does this imply that you made it from scratch? For example, if you bought the crust and just made the filling, can we still fairly say it's "home made"?

What about when you see "home made" on a menu? In food industry language, isn't "restaurant" the opposite of "home"?

Meaning, if the pie was made "on the premises", then that's not "home made", is it?

This brings to mind a dialogue in Alice in Wonderland, by Lewis Carrol.

"I don't know what you mean by 'glory'" Alice said.

Humpty Dumpty smiled contemptuously. "Of course you don't—till I tell you. I meant 'there's a nice knock-down argument for you!'"

"But 'glory' doesn't mean 'a nice knock-down argument'," Alice objected.

"When I use a word", Humpty Dumpty said, in rather a scornful tone, "it means just what I choose it to mean—neither more nor less."

"The question is," said Alice, "whether you can make words mean so many different things."

"The question is," said Humpty Dumpty, "which is to be master—that's all."

Look: if the pie is good I don't care where it came from. But I do think words should mean something. If we get in the habit of using them in the wrong places, we'll follow Humpty Dumpty's fate. And not even all the king's horses and all the king's men will be able to put things back together again.

Everyone Is In A Bad Mood

I slept badly yesterday and woke up feeling out of sorts.

My whole day was off after that. Boyfriend and I, terse; a tense encounter with a woman on the street, a grouchy bus driver.

It seemed like everyone was in a bad mood.

Wait a minute.

Every single person I had come across—everyone—had one thing in common.

Me.

We don't see the world as it is, we see the world as we are.

For everyone to get along we first need to extinguish our internal bonfires, stop seeing in others the projections of the storms we carry inside.

If we could become aware of everything we travel with we would quickly see that we are all much more the same than we are different.

Gut Instinct

When it comes to decision-making you have a big toolbox at your disposal.

Some of the tools in this box are:

Your intellect.

Data.

The opinions of people you respect.

Your gut instinct.

All of these tools are quite trusty but they're human and as such they are fallible.

(Even when the person that you trust giving you a valuable opinion sounds really authoritative and certain and is getting mad at you for not doing what they want you to do. An example that comes to mind is John Lennon's aunt and parental guardian saying *"A guitar is all right, John, but you'll never earn your living by it."* It was sage advice, and she would have been right under ordinary circumstances.)

The more you use these tools the better you understand how to balance them with each other and how to use them optimally.

(Although they can still fail you. Unfortunately no one can ever guarantee infallibility.)

Most of the tools available to you originate outside of you.

This means that if you follow them, someone else is dictating your life.

Your gut is at your core. It's *you* dictating your life.

If you listen to your gut, for better or worse (sometimes worse) your life becomes your own.

That decision maybe was a mistake, but it was all mine.

It's not that your gut instinct is infallible.

It's that listening to it is, at least for me, the only way to live.

How To Get Your Shit Together

Life isn't linear.

Life is not a straight path from chaos to order. It's not a *"I'm a catastrophe now, but I'll get my shit together and then live happily ever after."*

Instead, life is a falling apart/coming back together/falling apart process that is repeated over and over.

Understanding this is important because it give you the (accurate) perspective that whatever you are going through is unlikely to last.

It gives you sea legs, makes you more alert, awake, flexible and so very grateful.

Welcome to life.

Here are the steps that work for me when I find myself needing to get back on track.

Exercise/get in shape/eat well. This might sound vapid, but it's critical. It makes me feel better about myself, it makes me healthier; but most of all, in the middle of a crisis or a transition where I don't know what end is up it gives me something tangible to focus on.

Quiet. When we're adrift the world is filled with noise. Only through being quiet I can hear what I am trying to tell myself.

Hearing yourself is the only way out.

Awareness. You need to name everything. *I am afraid. I am lost. I am not where I want to be. I am in the wrong life.*

I did a terrible, terrible thing.

Awareness is so vital that every process proven to getting someone back on track begins with this simple step. *"My name is Dave, and I am an alcoholic."*

Trust. Remember when I said that things are unlikely to last? Believing that the chaos you find yourself in is temporary is helpful in the path back. Trust that.

Why Do We Misunderstand Each Other?

I have been held up at gunpoint twice.

I am hyper-aware of my surroundings, avoid walking alone at night, and get nervous if someone walks right towards me.

This morning I got on a crowded bus and saw a man push in my direction. He put his hand deep into his jacket and my brain yelled *OH MY GOD A GUN* a fraction of a second before my eyes saw him pull a cell phone out of his pocket.

If the man had said something innocuous to me, such as *"What time is it?"*, I might have stood there frozen in fear. I might have jumped out of the bus while it was still in motion.

This overreaction would have been related to my past experiences and not even remotely to him.

We are destined to misunderstand each other because our view of the world is corrupted by our baggage, our experiences, our assumptions, our expectations.

This is why it's important to work relentlessly to remain aware.

Even then we are not wired to perceive objective truth; only flashes of an often beautiful, mostly delusional interpretation.

Life is a house of mirrors, a comedy of errors, prejudiced, inexact.

This is why every single thing we do matters so very much. It is all we will ever see.

The Best

I have a need to be the best.

This characteristic makes me happy. It makes me feel driven, motivated, inspired.

I derive real pleasure from putting all my effort into everything I do, even when I'm the only one who could possibly know.

Except, sometimes it makes me miserable.

Sometimes needing to be the best makes me feel discouraged and exhausted and small. It makes me feel inadequate.

It makes me wish I could take a break from being me.

You see, my strengths are also my weaknesses.

You should never let go of anything that you are.

In getting rid of the worst of you, you would throw out the best of you.

What you need is to set it in the right place, where it can better serve you.

People Pleaser

Imagine you don't like pizza. The guy you are dating really likes it so you say you love pizza to make him like you.

You don't like pizza and end up eating pizza often rather than speaking up.

You risk ending up angry at him for always picking pizza.

Your anger builds up. You can't see it now but you are not angry at him. You are angry at yourself.

This is people pleasing.

Now imagine you don't like pizza and all your friends like it. You say you don't like pizza, but you like spending time with them so decide that you can be flexible, that this time you can set your preferences aside to be accommodating.

That's being nice.

I understand how this can be a fine line but the first will make you feel used and resentful and diminished and the second will make you happy because you own where you stand and are being generous.

People pleasing is not about making things easier for others but rather involves compromising who you are. It means trying to make everyone happy at your expense and realizing that despite your effort it cannot be done.

It's a losing battle to play against yourself.

It's sacrificing you to such an extent you lose track of who you are.

That's not nice. Nice begins by being nice to yourself.

Stand There And Take It

Have you noticed how people don't know how to take a compliment?

Try saying *"That is a beautiful sweater!"* or *"That presentation was really good!"* or *"You look gorgeous!"*

I see so frequently people who don't let the compliment in. *"What, this old thing?" "Oh, nonsense. That was nothing." "Oh, shut up!"*

But, what about criticism?

We believe that immediately.

It brings us down.

We open the door wide for the bad. Shut the door for the good.

This is preposterous.

Consider that words, thoughts, intentions become reality, and they add up. And what they add up to is our perception of who we are.

I propose that we all resolve to take compliments in. Don't shun them. Don't bat them back. Don't lessen them. Don't shake your head.

Stand there and take it.

And then say *"Thank you."*

Things To Let Go Of

Worry and guilt, because they accomplish nothing.

Blame. It doesn't absolve.

The impulse to be cruel.

Taking things personally.

Any claim that I am not enough.

Trying to change myself to please someone and, conversely—

Trying to change another person into what I think is best.

The feeling that everyone has it figured out except for me.

The sense that I have to live up to another person's expectations.

Whatever anybody is saying about me, and, conversely—

The urge to gossip.

Lies. And, no, they are never "necessary". No one needs their truth "managed".

Control. You can't "make" anyone do anything.

How To Be A Good Friend

Here are three simple tips to being a good friend:

Letting another person be your friend on her terms and not yours. People love you how they love you, not how you want to be loved.

Example: I am very punctual. I have a friend who is never on time. I interpreted this as a lack of respect and interest. She did not care enough.

But her being late has more to do with her own idiosyncrasy than her feelings about me.

Accepting your friends for who they are rather than providing judgement or opinions on the choices that they make. Don't "fix" or "improve" them or show them why your way is better. It isn't.

Example: Aside from an occasional glass of Prosecco to toast a special occasion, I hardly ever drink. I don't like alcohol. Most of my friends drink.

We let each other be.

Showing up. Your friend will have "defining moments" that you need to be there for to the best of your ability. It's so easy to say no when things get inconvenient.

Example: Is a friend of yours getting married in another city? Of course it would be easier not to go. When you look back on your life you will see the extra effort was worth it.

Transference

"Transference" is a term first coined by Sigmund Freud and later used by others, such as Carl Jung, and is defined as:

"The redirection of feelings from one person to another."

Have you ever been attracted to someone because they remind you of someone else?

Have you found yourself liking (or intensely disliking) a teacher and realizing later he is just like your father?

How many times have you felt your girlfriend treats you like your mother?

Does an argument with a friend make you irrationally angry, only to realize you are replicating a discussion you frequently have with another family member?

Transference happens all the time, and is often present in a dynamic where one person holds a position of authority.

People "fall in love" with their instructors, their teachers, their therapists.

Anyone who is looked up to—from a yoga teacher to a psychoanalyst to a therapist—should know about transference and how to handle it, as getting romantically involved with a student or patient is a breach of ethics.

It takes advantage of someone in a vulnerable position.

For the person feeling all these feelings, transference can be a powerful tool, as it offers a way to "work through" things that have been hard to deal with (you are feeling love, anger, sexual attraction towards a near-stranger rather than a main character in your life).

Transference casts things in a different light and as such allows you to better understand yourself.

Being aware that it exists helps you avoid the pitfalls of pursuing a relationship with someone who is just a reflection of someone else.

Mindfulness/Flow

Imagine, if you will, that I am sitting behind my computer writing and I have before me a big bowl of popcorn.

I am eating the popcorn and trying to focus on my writing but can't because I am reaching out for more popcorn.

Wait a minute I think. *I am not really concentrating on the writing, and not really enjoying the popcorn.*

I push my computer aside, pull the bowl towards me and decide to grant myself the joy of eating the popcorn while doing nothing else.

This is mindfulness.

Being fully there for my crunchy bowl of popcorn.

If, conversely, I say to myself *Whoa. This delicious popcorn is distracting me from my writing!* and I push the bowl away and write and eventually become so absorbed in what I'm trying to describe that I forget about the popcorn, forget about my sore shoulders, forget that I'm already late for where I need to be next, forget about making dinner, *feel like I could just sit here and write all day*, that's flow.

Worry

I used to think worrying was a character trait, but I now realize it's something I inadvertently practiced and accidentally enforced.

I did this because I was under the impression that worrying somehow protected the people that I loved; and because I felt it "prepared" me for the worst.

It's instead the biggest possible waste of time.

It's envisioning all the things you don't want to see happen.

It's allowing anxiety to win.

I will now reveal one of my greatest discoveries: worry is a habit, and as such, you can break it.

Like any habit, this is hard and takes time but it's worth it.

Instead of obsessing over what is worrying you, replace it with a positive thought.

What if I do badly in my next presentation?

But, what if it turns out amazing?

Both scenarios are equally plausible, but the first one robs me of the present moment, and the second one helps me envision what I'd like to see happen.

I'd rather practice that instead.

Advice For Women (or anyone)

You are not half of anything. You were created whole.

Find your voice. Don't apologize *(Ummm, I'm sorry but...)*. Don't hesitate *(should I say it or not?)*. Don't minimize *(I know this is probably really silly but...)*. Don't use needless words *(I mean, like, well, I think that...)*. Speak up.

You don't need anything other than you. You don't need a man. You have yourself. I'm not saying men aren't wonderful (because they are!) or that they are not worth your time (yes they are!). What I'm saying is that no one is worth giving up you.

Never underestimate the friendship of another woman. Don't create rivalries; shun jealousy and competition and accept your friends for who they are, free of judgement. Help other women up. Women friends are invaluable. They are your tribe.

You are more powerful than you think. Don't give that power away. It belongs to you.

Instructions On What To See

If you believe something is not possible, that something is out of your reach, you will look for confirmation that what you believe is true.

Your brain is trying to defend what it thinks, so proof of the opposite of what it thinks will be discarded.

In other words, your brain actively deletes any alternative because it wants to confirm that whatever you believe in is true.

For example, I used to believe that I couldn't afford to quit my job.

This belief was Truth to me and I argued to defend it.

I actually defended something that made me feel trapped and anxious.

The day I decided to resign my reality changed. I wanted quitting to be viable and every day a new path opened before me.

A path that had been there all along.

You always have choices. You often, without knowing that you are doing so, refuse to see them.

Your attitude gives your brain instructions on what to see.

This is why it's important to come at things from a place of receptivity and peace rather than from a place of stress. *"What is it that I am not seeing?"* is so much better than *"OH MY GOD THERE IS NO WAY OUT."*

You cannot be too optimistic, unless you think you can.

In which case you will prove to yourself that you are right.

Love At Thirteen

I am 47 and in love and this love is such an important part of my life but isn't all of it.

I love other things too that deserve my attention, my interest, my time.

When I was thirteen oh my god all I wanted was to be left alone so I could think of him. If the phone rang (this was the time of landlines and no cell phones) I ran to see who it was *please get off the phone mom get off the phone I am expecting a very important call.*

If he said *hello* I'd spend all of recess calibrating what his hello could have possibly meant. I mimicked his inflection to make sure the exhaustive analysis yielded accurate results.

Could it mean that he liked me?

If he said (and he said) *I like it when you wear black* I wore black every day. *I like AC/DC* meant memorizing the lyrics to all the songs.

To this day I still salute all those about to rock.

If a thirteen year old told me today she was in love I would know her head was swimming in it, her heart drowning in it, so I'd take her seriously and take the whole afternoon off to discuss with her at length, in depth, the one thousand possible meanings of his hello.

Wait. Tell me again exactly. How. He. Said. It.

I'd take her seriously because all feelings are serious, because I respect the person for feeling them, and because I feel honored she shared with me such a sacred, intimate thing.

And because love is love, at any age.

How To Screw Up Your Life

Whatever you try, make certain you get it perfect.

Lie to people in order to please or "protect" them so that they can never distinguish who you are or what you really want.

Nag the people that you love.

Do only what you are already comfortable doing.

Focus your time and energy on living up to everyone's expectations.

Resolve to never risk failure.

Do what doesn't work over and over.

Expect a lot from others. Bonus points if you don't tell them what that is. Because, they should know, right?

Hold on to heavy things: toxic relationships, a job you don't love, stuff you don't need.

Dwell on negative thoughts, particularly hatred. Hate yourself.

Conclude you are much safer if you trust no one.

Conclude you are much safer if you love no one.

Trigger

Sometimes I see betrayal where there isn't any.

I interpret certain actions as a form of betrayal because I was lied to in the past and my brain has installed this hyper-sensitive trigger designed to keep me safe.

It's called a defense mechanism, and it's faulty because it makes me push away people who, while dealing with their own issues, have no intention of deliberately hurting me.

If you resolve to react to your defense mechanism rather than to the truth, you end up pushing everyone away.

You take your sensitive trigger into every relationship, fighting with different people for the same reasons.

No one on Earth can live up to the unrealistic demands of our terrified defense mechanisms.

The trigger needs to be adjusted to be fair (which is easier said than done).

I decided to adjust mine the day I realized it was better to be unsafe than to lose the people that I loved for reasons that didn't exist.

Go Somewhere

Most humans crave routine. It keeps us efficient, organized and ultimately comfortable.

Too much routine for too long makes us numb. It's hard to notice things you see every day, hard to challenge yourself with all the things you do over and over.

When everything is on automatic a part of your brain switches off.

Breaking the routine—making yourself uncomfortable—is key to learning, to feeling more alive, and to being receptive. It wakes you up.

It changes you.

This means trying out new things. It means doing things you might not be good at. It means playing with being incompetent, setting your ego aside to let the world in.

Travel is a good way to make all this happen. You are in an unfamiliar place, where everything—your surroundings, the language, the food, the time of day—is different.

You become more receptive.

It changes your vantage point, in effect forcing you to see things from a new perspective. You begin to understand things more clearly and maybe change your point of view.

You renew your life force through increased curiosity. You invite serendipity.

What you are experiencing is so revitalizing that you make it easier to live in the present and leave the future for later, where it belongs.

Discomfort. Being off balance. Experimenting. Experiencing awe.

Lose yourself to find yourself.

Lack Of Trust

Not trusting anyone means moving through your life handicapped by your own insecurities.

It means never giving anyone else—not even yourself—a fighting chance.

It means being forever emotionally unavailable, attributing to people who love you betrayals that never took place.

It means seeing every relationship you hold end for the same reasons, the same fights playing out over and over, a sad, repetitive, exhausting infinite loop.

The day you resolve to trust again you do so because you realize that trusting and getting hurt is a lot less painful than consistently pushing away anyone who loves you.

How To Stop Taking Things Personally

You get on the bus. You accidentally bump into a man. He puts his face right next to yours and yells.

"You are a fucking idiot! Watch where you put your feet, you moron!"

It's hard not to take this personally. He's yelling in your face. He's calling you names. He looks like he might get violent.

You don't know this, but that man was laid off from a job he had been working on for over two decades. He has been trying to get another one, but he can't catch a break. He's worried about providing for his family. He walks around trying to fill his days, feeling useless, invisible.

Him yelling at you had nothing to do with you.

The guy (or girl) you are dating doesn't trust you. He keeps his distance, plays it safe. You try to be worthy of his trust but it doesn't seem to make a difference.

You don't know this, but before he met you he was badly hurt. He's been cheated on, lied to, betrayed. His trust issues are his to resolve. They have nothing to do with you.

You begin to learn that nothing is personal when you understand that people have a history that began before they encountered you. When you can see they are hiding behind walls, tall, solid walls originally erected to protect themselves.

Other people's walls are not your problem.

Which is a good thing, because dealing with your own is a full time job.

Advisor

Fear is an excellent quality, designed by evolution to keep you safe.

It takes its responsibility extremely seriously. If it were up to it, you would say no to everything.

It wants to make absolutely certain no harm can come to you.

Except there is no such thing, so if all you did was listen to it your world would progressively shrink.

You would reach the point where you'd begin to fear things that don't exist, because fear, when fed, becomes insatiable. It can never keep you safe enough.

There are so many things to experience in the world that are the absolute essence of life. Things that, I'm sorry to tell you, are pretty much guaranteed to hurt. Love, friendship, relationships, risks, adventures, failure.

Going through life trying to avoid pain is the same as going through life being guided only by fear.

Accept instead that you are going to get hurt.

Keep fear as an advisor. Not the boss.

If you make decisions based on only the voice of fear your life will steer off course quickly, and become increasingly dull, grey, bleak, diminished, empty.

Now, that's something to be afraid of.

Different From Me

It's early Sunday morning and I'm sitting at my computer. Boyfriend is sound asleep. He won't be up for at least another couple of hours. I can't stay in bed after 7:00.

The house is strewn with his stuff. Boots under the dining room table, jeans on the couch, and piles of random collections: keys, coins, receipts. I am neat. I clear surfaces.

For breakfast I will maybe have an apple with muesli or a couple of scrambled eggs. He'll have leftovers: pork confit, roast chicken. He is a carnivore. I'm not a vegetarian but have never before him considered buying anything "bone in".

Boyfriend does CrossFit. I do yoga. After exercising he wants a burger. I want juice.

He's social, has friends to see and parties to go to. I love my friends but would rather stay home. Boyfriend exerts no pressure on me but is definitely an unintentional motivator in getting me out of the house. When we're out I don't drink. He likes Manhattans.

In the early evening (9:00 pm) I'm winding down (also known as struggling to remain awake). Boyfriend finds things to do. He doesn't come to bed before midnight.

Being with someone different from you is hard work. You argue more. Sometimes in the middle of the argument you realize with horror that you're wrong, that you've been wrong for years.

You see things you have never seen before, in particular about yourself.

You respect another person for who they are. You relinquish the effort of trying to change someone else.

You more clearly identify your own boundaries. You become more of who you are.

In a very real way this sets you free.

Boyfriend has affected my perspective of the world with his own. Through adjusting to our differences he has widened my views. He has changed me.

It is not and never will be an easy relationship, but I am a better person for having found him.

Blind Spot

We all—every one of us—exhibit patterns of behavior that are obvious to everyone but that we ourselves cannot see.

We will deny that they exist.

These are our "blind spots". Carl Jung calls them our "shadow".

Have you ever noticed how you are often involved in situations that are similar across different aspects of your life?

Why does everyone leave me?

Or how you have the exact same fight with different people in different relationships?

Have you ever said—or heard a friend say—things like *"Why does every person I date end up cheating on me?"* or *"Why does everyone betray me?"* or *"Why doesn't anyone understand me?"* or *"Why do I always end up in long distance relationships?"*

These are all the consequence of our blind spots.

"Until you make the unconscious conscious," said Jung, *"it will direct your life, and you will call it fate."*

Being Yourself

Imagine that someone with the best of intentions gives you a pair of shoes.

You put them on and they are too tight.

Not only that. They are the wrong style for your uniquely shaped feet.

You take a few steps and your toes begin to hurt.

You decide not to say anything.

What if you offend the person who gave you the shoes?

What if they decide they don't like you anymore?

Have you ever worn uncomfortable shoes? Let me tell you. No matter how much you want them to fit, after a few hours you can no longer pretend.

Taking them off and wearing the right shoes will transform your life.

Your feet, rather than blistered, bleeding, eventually permanently damaged, will feel like they grew wings.

A pair of shoes right for you will take you to places you now can only dream of.

Even when you really want to, you cannot go through life pretending to be something you are not.

The earlier you change into the right pair of shoes the better.

Disinterested Friend

When I was little—maybe 11—I wanted to be friends with a girl who never seemed particularly interested in being my friend.

At my (inexplicable) insistence, we spent a lot of time together but the effort I put into the relationship was definitely one-sided.

One afternoon at her house I woke up to the fact that she always treated me with a bit of disinterest, even disdain.

I told her it was time for me to go home and never called her again.

She never called me either.

Very shortly after I started hanging out with a girl who seemed happy to hang out with me. The friendship was effortless and natural. We remain in contact to this day, decades later.

Trying to force a relationship of any nature with someone who exhibits reluctance or a lack of enthusiasm for you is likely to set the tone for how the entire relationship is going to be. Lukewarm, disinterested, leaving me with the feeling that I somehow would never be enough.

I can't help but feel I deserve better than that.

If instead I invest time and effort in relationships with people who are just as enthusiastic about me as I am about them, I experience every day what it's like to be loved for who I already am.

The secret in decoding who you should try to approach cannot be found in the behavior of the other person.

It lies within you asking yourself what it is that you want: to be loved instantly and enthusiastically, or to struggle forever to meet someone's invisible expectations?

The Best Of Me

It's so hard to attempt to change for another.

It's easy to feel you are compromising yourself.

When the dynamics of a relationship are pushing me to change, I ask myself one thing.

Who is it that I want to be?

Do I want, for example, to be petty, insecure, nagging, demanding, rapacious? Do I want to feel in the cavity of my chest a tightening, a grasping, despair? Do I want to live with the acerbity that arises from trying unsuccessfully to make another person do what I think they should do?

Or do I want to feel increasingly free, expansive, independent; clear on my own pursuits and interests, strong?

I don't change for others. I change for myself.

This means that every opportunity to love is also an opportunity for me to become a better person, to exercise my character in a new way.

I don't become resentful because whatever it is that I decide to do I am doing it for me.

This isn't selfish. It's giving. Give others the best of you.

How To Feel More Grateful

Gratitude has the power to change the course of your life.

It shifts your perspective, and therefore your reality. It demonstrates that you are enough, that you have enough. It exercises optimism.

It gets you out of the confines of your head.

Gratitude is like a muscle. You can develop it to have more of it.

I begin with silence. It helps quiet down my thoughts and allows me to hear myself feel.

At the very beginning of the day, I look around and say specific thank-yous. They might begin obvious and ordinary.

Thank you for the smell of coffee. Thank you for toast. Thank you so much for avocado, for my notebook, for my pencil, for my time, for this sunny morning I have given myself. Thank you for my life.

Thank you for my disproportionate good fortune. Thank you for love.

If you are having a difficult day, or a difficult moment, say thank you. Yep. It sucks. It's hard. You can do it through gritted teeth. *Thank you. Thank you for this client who cancelled the session after all the preparation work had been done.*

Thank you for the lesson, because although I now feel like I wasted time, I know how to avoid this in the future.

If you are angry say thank you. *Thank you Boyfriend for our fights. Thank you for all the things you teach me about myself. Thank you for reminding me that sometimes we speak in different languages. Thank you for the time you spend trying to decipher mine; mercurial, effervescent.*

At the end of the day, say thank you. For the day, for the good parts and the bad, for beauty and all the good things that hide inside bad things.

Say thank you for absurd things, ridiculous things, small things, glorious every day things you take for granted.

Thank you for the way sunlight catches the leaves of the tree outside. Thank you for the curve of that white bowl and for the refrigerator and my orange cushion.

Thank you for my family and thank you for my friends and thank you for my new pillows.

Thank you for insomnia because I can steal looks of Boyfriend while he sleeps.

"Wear gratitude like a cloak," said Rumi, "and it will feed every corner of your life."

Increased Responsibility

Boyfriend is late.

He said he would be home at 8:00 p.m. but just texted me to let me know he was still at work.

I am on time. I had to make changes to my day in order to be home and ready by 8:00 like we agreed.

Him being late is a reflection of the fact he does not respect my time. It means our date is not as important as whatever he is doing.

Wait a minute, Dushka. That's just not true. You are taking this personally. It's not about you. It's about him.

Boyfriend has been working hard. He has taken on increased responsibility. For him to be late means he is buried under a pile of things to do. It means he must be under a lot of pressure.

He would not choose to be late. He'd want to be home on time, just like I would prefer to go out on a date with him rather than having to work late.

This could have ended in an absurd fight, with me angry and feeling like I don't matter, with him stressed and feeling like I don't understand.

I can let my thoughts control me (and sometimes they do), but my life is better when I take a few breaths and guide them instead.

What Is It Like To Have No Control?

I've often wondered how on Earth I can protect the people that I love. I really don't want them to get hurt.

Please, please be careful.

But I can't. I don't have that kind of power.

Or, when someone does something that hurts me, I want them to stop.

Please don't make me jealous.

But jealousy is inside me and as such only I am responsible for it. No one makes me do or feel anything. Only I can do that.

So many good/bad things can happen. Earthquakes and accidents and, well, Boyfriend could stop loving me.

Let me just break the news directly: life is unpredictable and any sense of control we have over anything at all is an illusion.

Even when my calendar is perfectly organized and my shoes are lined up and my sweaters are folded and my cabinets are dust free and my dresses are sorted by color.

Which is to say you already know what it's like to have no control, because regardless of what you might believe today the truth is neither you nor I have any.

You should also know you come perfectly equipped to handle whatever comes your way.

Safety does not reside in the fallacy of having control.

It comes with realizing you will manage just fine without it.

How Did My Parents' Divorce Affect Me?

There is only one way to know this for sure: if I had another me in a parallel life, without divorced parents. What would she be like? How would she be different from me?

She would have grown up in a house where everyone was fighting and everyone was unhappy and everyone felt trapped. How would that have impacted her way of looking at the world?

And how long and to what degree can we point to our environment as a reason behind who we are and how we regard things?

Is there not more work and grit and power in assuming full responsibility?

The Moon And The Stars

When I was in my late teens the guys I tended to go for were players. I was drawn to their charisma, their charm, their sense of humor, their social ease and the grandiose declarations of love and improbable promises.

Who doesn't want the moon and all the stars?

After a few weeks of dating I'd find out the guy was promising the moon to others with equal fervor and we'd break up, him contrite riding off into the sunset, me in a river of tears.

It's really hard to feel wronged and find blame in your own behavior. I wasn't doing the cheating. I was in fact vigilant, ever suspicious, in an effort to reduce the chances of this happening again.

Except the way out is never in attempting to have an impact over another person's behavior. The way out is inside myself.

Why did every guy I date cheat on me? How could this possibly be my fault?

Blame at first can feel liberating, but it's a trap.

If something is not your fault, it's not your responsibility.

If it's not your responsibility, there is nothing you can do.

If there is nothing you can do, you secure your own powerlessness.

If you are powerless you delude yourself into thinking there is no way out. You are then destined to make the same mistakes.

If I find a way to make myself responsible, I find the key.

And I need that key because I really don't want to do this anymore.

What do the guys cheating on me have in common?

Me.

Who chooses them, is attracted to them?

Me.

Can I figure out a way to not be attracted to them? Or, be attracted to them but not act upon that attraction, choose instead equally attractive men more compatible with the fact that I am monogamous?

Of course this changes if something happens to me that I truly have no control over (such as being the victim of a crime).

But in a general sense finding responsibility within you *(what am I missing? How am I contributing to this?)* instead of pointing the finger at someone else is the only way to find out how powerful you are, how free to change the patterns you are convinced hold you captive.

Shapeshifting Is Not A Superpower

If you can transform into absolutely anything, you lose track of who you are.

If you lose track of who you are you don't know what side you're on or why.

If you lose track of who you are you forget what you stand for.

Where Are All The Good Guys?

Today was a really hot day in San Francisco. I went on a hike with a friend. He's really shy and doesn't talk much. He's a good listener and always remembers exactly what I told him when we last spoke.

After our walk we went into a coffee shop and stood in line to order something refreshing. *"Dushka, why don't you go sit down?"* he asked. *"Tell me what you want and I'll bring it to you."* He showed up at my table a few minutes later with a huge glass of fresh lemonade and set it before me. He would not let me pay him for it.

Boyfriend is going to get a beer tonight with a friend. I know him. He's thoughtful and interesting and has a strong point of view and whenever we hang out together I wonder how it is that despite his efforts he's still single.

I understand the frustration in looking for something you cannot seem to find. I know that saying there are no good guys out there can ring true on a bleak night.

I want to point out the opposite is just as true.

Believe me when I tell you good guys are everywhere.

Possessed

The etymology of the word "enthusiasm" is one of my favorites.

The word "enthusiasm" comes from the Greek *enthusiasmos,* a variant of *entheos.*

It means "to be possessed by a God" or "to have a God within".

I believe we owe it to ourselves to go through life possessed; passionately absorbed in what interests us.

Every time I don't feel this way I realize I have strayed from what matters to me and I have to go find it.

Being Honest Versus Complaining

Imagine a nail and a wall.

Honesty takes the nail and holds it up against the wall.

With the other hand it grabs a hammer and bangs the nail clean into the wall.

Complaining takes the nail and holds it up against everything. With the other hand it grabs the hammer and taps the nail on the bookcase, on the dining room table, on the floor, on its thumb.

Complaining scatters a lot of sputtering energy. It dents, damages, scratches, pits, nicks, perforates, but ultimately accomplishes nothing.

In the end, complaining is too tired and frustrated to do what it takes to appropriately drive the nail into the wall.

Honesty has already hung a beautiful painting and has moved on from ever dealing with that nail and that wall again.

Ultimatum

An ultimatum is a threat. No one responds well to being threatened.

It's a form of manipulation that tends to happen when nothing else has worked, which means that the person hurling it is coming from a place of powerlessness.

This reminds me of a scene in a movie with Clint Eastwood. A character is relishing the thought of killing another and finally finds him in a vulnerable position (taking a bath).

He smirks and begins to chatter on and on about how long he has waited for this moment.

The guy in the bathtub pulls a gun out from the soapy water and kills him.

"If you're going to shoot, shoot," he says. *"Don't talk."*

Small Decisions

Every day I make hundreds of decisions.

Some are (almost) a given. (*Should I get out of bed?*)

Some are somewhat obsessive or charged with everyday angst. (*How much time will I need to get to my meeting? What time should I leave? Should I take the bus? Should I take a cab?*)

Many of them are unconscious, to the point that I forget if I made them at all. *(Wait. Did I take my medicine already? Did I just brush my teeth, or not? Where are we? Did I just miss my bus stop?)*

Going through each day more *aware* of the small decisions that I make tends to have a big impact (on both my day and my life).

It requires that I do one thing at a time, remain present, even change things up so my brain cannot switch to automatic.

A different bus route home, having something unusual for lunch so I can appreciate the food instead of letting my mind wander.

Saying yes to work that requires travel so I can wake up in an entirely different city and see everything with new eyes.

If life is the sum of our decisions I want to make more of them on purpose.

An Invisible Prison

If you are attached to getting everything perfect the effort will generate more anxiety than joy.

It will imply you never try anything new.

That you don't trust yourself to be bad at something.

Perfectionism will shrink your world. It's an invisible prison.

"I am a perfectionist" to me means *"I will have a hard time admitting I make mistakes, and therefore I will learn very slowly."*

Perfectionism is not a character flaw—it's a habit. We pick it up because we have been taught it's a virtue, but look at it. It has less to do with excellence and more to do with insecurity.

Ambition is a form of hunger. Perfection is a form of fear.

Perfectionism is paralyzing. Once we realize this we can practice letting it go.

Sometimes, good enough is good enough.

Always, you are good enough.

Is Ego Good Or Bad?

I went to a really difficult yoga class this morning.

The teacher was giving us multilevel options for some of the most advanced poses so that we could do the pose that better suited each one of us.

If I am "level one" in a certain pose and "level two" option is explained, my brain whispers *"YEAH! Let's do that instead!"*

To which the other voice in my brain says *"Hmmm, no. You can't do that yet."*

To which she insists *"Yes we can! Let's just try!"*

This internal debate is at the heart of why I regard the world with enthusiasm. Why pushing myself comes naturally to me.

But, what about taking care of myself? How many times have I gotten injured for attempting to do something my body is not ready for?

How many times do I get in trouble for biting off more than I can chew?

Many. Many times.

The ego likes attention. It wants to be loved, admired, appreciated. It loves praise.

My ego is neither bad nor good. My ego is neutral. It depends on the place that I give it when I make decisions.

If I let it be my advisor it will always encourage me, push me, ignore what I can't do. I always want an advisor like that.

If I let the ego be my master I will make the wrong decisions for the wrong reasons and nothing I do or have will ever be enough.

You Can't Miss Out If You're Doing Exactly What You Want

The older I get the more I realize I don't know what I want. Keeping my options open, rather than feeling like I have to decide, determine, label or choose, has considerably improved my life.

That being said, I'm very clear on what I *don't* want. Even if what I don't want might create internal tension.

Here is an example.

I am an introvert and go out of my way to avoid parties. I love my friends but most frequently want to be home (or with small groups of people).

Then I find out someone threw a party and didn't invite me and feel left out.

I let myself feel whatever I'm feeling but, hey. I don't like parties. If the price of not having to go to one is feeling a teeny bit excluded I sit peacefully with that.

The feeling soon dissipates.

You learn to be more comfortable with the notion you are missing out when you know you are exactly where you want to be.

You can't "miss out" on something you are not interested in doing.

The antidote to FOMO is finding yourself.

Please Change For Me

When I met Boyfriend he and his women friends greeted each other with a peck on the lips.

I find kissing people on the mouth intensely personal. This habit of his made me uncomfortable.

I told him so, and he was baffled. He said to him it meant nothing. He didn't notice he was doing it.

If for him it was nothing and for me it was intimate and painful, I reasoned, asking him to stop made sense. So I did.

I said: "*Please stop kissing women on the mouth.*"

He heard: "*I want to control you.*"

I meant: "*Please don't hurt me.*"

He said: "*I'm not going to stop. You can't control what I do.*"

I heard: "*I could not care less if this makes you uncomfortable. I don't love you enough to adjust my behavior.*"

Looking back, my approach was wrong. It was wrong because the discomfort was my issue, to deal with within myself.

I should have said *"this is how it makes me feel"* but instead said *"I want your behavior to change to accommodate me."*

The difference might seem subtle but how we word things has an impact.

Language between lovers is fragile. What we say is not always interpreted in the way that we think.

If Boyfriend asked me to change something about myself I might hear *"I don't love you just the way you are. I need you to change a few things so I can find you beautiful."*

I'd suggest that he go find the woman of his dreams.

How To Conquer Fear

There is so much I want to do.

I set my alarm clock every day for 6:00 a.m.

On most mornings I'm awake before it even rings, but sometimes I'm sound asleep and all I want is to hit the snooze button.

The snooze button is so delicious. It lures me. It beckons me. It's like a siren call.

Mmmmm a bit more sleep. Please just a little bit.

If I asked you *"How can I resist the snooze button!? Give me tips! Give me a methodology! I need a plan!"*

You'd say *"There is only one step. One way. Get up."*

This too is the case with fear. There is no recipe. No trick. No short cut.

No way to not feel it.

Feel fear. Do it anyway.

How Do Lovers Who Speak Different Languages Understand Each Other?

Before you learned to speak, language was foreign to you.

You learned to pair words with meaning, like "bed" or "truck".

But you also grasped abstract concepts, like "imagine", "think", or "hope".

If I tell you I woke up this morning "yearning" for something I cannot describe, you would understand.

You even comprehend and know how to use words like "the".

If you read a sentence and found in the midst of it a word you had never seen before you would probably correctly infer its meaning.

Let's take it one step further.

Helen Keller was born deaf, mute and blind. She "spoke" her first word when she was seven.

Anne Sullivan, her teacher—maybe one of the greatest teachers mankind has ever known—came into her life when she was six.

When Helen's parents asked what she would teach her, she said *"Language"*, because *"language is to the mind more than light is to the eye."*

She spelled words into her hand through sign language for a full year before Helen grasped there was such a thing as "language", before she understood everything had a word.

Her first word was "water".

Helen Keller went on to speak, write, understand; she became a writer and lecturer.

This is also what happens when lovers born in different countries learn each other's language. They grasp all the things you can touch, like "skin", like "nose", like "eyelash", like "heart".

Then, with just a bit more work, letting the brain do what it does, "wonder", "absolution", "miracle".

The Jungle That Is My Brain

Imagine a jungle, verdant, lush, thick with vegetation.

You come along with a machete and painstakingly, laboriously clear a path to walk on.

You use it every day, back and forth, and slowly realize this path of yours, while well trodden, is not ideal.

If you had known then what you know now you might have chosen a flatter, easier route, one with a better view, less fraught with risk.

You realize this, but know an alternate path does not currently exist.

You would have to grab that machete and begin again the arduous work of clearing a new way.

This takes monumental effort. Not just because it's difficult but because it feels counterintuitive.

Better to use the existing path, despite the evidence that another could be better.

When you do things a certain way—habits, routines, beliefs, proclivities, assumptions—you are in effect carving out a pathway in your brain.

Repetition makes it wider, more comfortable.

Creating a new path doesn't feel natural—it doesn't even feel possible—and as such you default again and again into the one you know.

It's who I am, you say. *The cross I have to bear. The cards I was dealt.*

It's my destiny.

This is why habits are hard to break, why we fall into patterns we know make us suffer but can't seem to redesign.

But we can.

We can determine what it is we want to build. We can do this if we remind ourselves how making the same mistake over and over is hurting us.

We can envision what a better way might look like if we decided once and for all to embrace the fact that if you are willing to put in the work there is always a better way.

Just because you believe you can't get there from here doesn't make it true.

The clearing of this new path would go slowly at first. We'd often be working in darkness, in the absence of faith, burdened by fatigue, sorrow or despair.

One day soon this new path, once unfathomable, unattainable, unimaginable, will be obvious, easy, wide and sunny.

This is how it's always possible to clear space for future behavior, better patterns, more intentional, more purposeful habits.

This is how we can set ourselves up to finally arrive at a better outcome.

Alternate Reality

She loves him and is heartbroken to realize he does not love her.

He is leaving, moving to another city for a job.

She cannot believe, after all they have been through, after all the promises, that he doesn't love her enough to stay.

The fact is he is leaving *because* he loves her. He wants to do better, do his part to provide for her and for the family they have spoken of having.

He cannot believe she does not love him enough to join him.

We each live in our personal alternate reality.

Only when we set aside our own interests can we travel to somebody else's.

Your Inner Hero

How often do you feel you need more sleep when the alarm goes off? You get up and get on with your day despite fatigue.

How many times do you resist lashing out at someone, hold in your frustration, your anger? How frequently do you make an effort to, rather than snap, react instead with compassion?

Have you felt you just want to be a better friend, a better parent, a better family member, a better spouse?

You do well one day and not so well another but marshall your forces and return to battle the next day.

How many times are you generous when no one is watching?

How many times do you emerge victorious from internal battles no one else can see?

I really admire big, flashy, single acts of heroism; but I also recognize the effort of rising to the occasion day in, day out.

The "every day" is relentless. It requires so much work.

Without diminishing the traditional definition of a hero, let's also recognize the small, ordinary hero inside each of us, who shows up every single day.

I Wish I'd Known This Sooner

I should have left my house at least half an hour earlier.

Now I am in a hurry, and running late stresses me terribly.

People around me wander, take their time, look around, stop and think.

Their rhythm, languid, is frustrating the heck out of me.

I want everyone to get out of my way.

Except, wanting or feeling something—even with despair or bluster—does not constitute another person's obligation.

The fact that I am in a hurry does not mean others have to move aside to accommodate me.

Just because I am convinced a stranger should be my friend doesn't suggest said stranger must correspond with equal enthusiasm.

If I have fallen madly in love with someone I gaze at from afar—or even with someone I am dating and know well—the person that I love is not required or bound to love me back.

If I am jealous, that does not oblige my significant other to stop having friends of the opposite gender.

My feelings—my incandescent, unsettling, agitated, dazzling, effulgent, raging feelings—are mine to sort out.

Expecting another person's behavior to accommodate my feelings is at best self-centered and disrespectful, at worst unhealthy, irrational, abusive.

To you, sending thirty four thoughtful messages a day to a stranger might be a generous, well intended display of wonder and affection.

To the unsuspecting recipient it is the very definition of harassment.

Forcing your feelings on another, aside from mad and disjointed, is the equivalent of squandering yourself.

You are causing yourself pain by acting delusional and wondering why the other person is stepping away from you instead of towards you.

If someone doesn't love you back they are not doing anything to you.

You are in effect breaking your own heart.

Realize instead your feelings belong to you. It is up to you to manage them, rein them in, contain them, hold them or rejoice in them.

So, yeah. I really wish I had known this sooner. Because I don't know about you, but this notion alone is enough to keep me busy forever.

Curiosity

Curiosity is expansive, related to life, truth and adaptation in the same way apathy and disinterest are related to internal extinction and darkness.

It's a form of hunger, avid, fervent, one of the vital ingredients in learning new things and being productive.

Its power defeats uncertainty and fear.

Curiosity renews us. It's through its drive that our life becomes richer and more varied. Curiosity stretches our intellect.

Curiosity and its close cousins (eagerness, interest, an inquisitive mind, a thirst for knowledge) are the original symptoms of success.

There is a direct correlation between curiosity and happiness.

Here is the best part: curiosity is not a character trait but a habit, and as such it can be cultivated.

A Healthy Relationship

You know that feeling of waking up in the morning with your heart full *I don't want to eat or sleep or do anything other than be with him is it time yet is it time yet?*

I know that feels like love. And I'm not saying it isn't.

But it's not healthy love.

Healthy love is not co-dependent. It's never *"the two of us are one."*

And, what about *"we never fight! Not ever!"*? That's not healthy either.

If you don't fight, you never establish boundaries. The solidity of the relationship is not put to the test.

In healthy relationships you occasionally fight. You fight well and you fight fair. You don't say *"all"* or *"never"* or *"always"*. You don't dredge up the past seventeen arguments. You are not intentionally hurtful—there are no low blows. You argue over the issue, rather than attack the person. You are specific. *"You hurt my feelings when you interrupted me"* rather than the dramatically sweeping *"You have no respect for who I am!"*

What about unconditional love? Unconditional love sounds deceptively romantic, but it's not healthy. Unconditional love equals no boundaries. Just like you need to treat each other with respect, you also need to respect yourself.

In healthy love, you are individuals, independent. There is no *"need".* You each have whole lives without the other: friends, interests, pursuits. This is not scary, because you trust. You trust yourself.

A healthy relationship is capable of evolution, because life is uncertain, because who you both are is in perpetual transformation, and because everything—everything—will change.

Your significant other will test your patience (sometimes a lot), will reveal where you need to grow, will inadvertently help you identify your boundaries.

You will be better for having him in your life.

He (or she) will be your accomplice—not your lifesaver, not your flotation device—in this magnificent, wild, erratic, inconstant, bewitching journey that is life.

Irrational Terror

Driving terrifies me.

While driving can definitely be dangerous I consider my fear irrational because of how it presents itself. It doesn't happen every time I drive, and when it does it comes like a wave of utter panic that takes my breath away.

While I really, really don't like driving, I am OK doing so around a city. The overwhelming, paralyzing sensation I am describing is something I feel mostly on highways.

The best way I can explain it is the illusion that the car is going to fall up (into the sky).

When someone else is driving I feel like other cars are much closer than they actually are. I have to resist yelling *"CAREFUL!"* at cars that are "closing in on us" but are really several lanes away.

I think a lot about fear. It's meant to protect us, but sometimes our instincts go into overdrive or our fear is displaced (for example, when I am under stress, my driving panic tends to get worse).

I tell myself that fear can be arbitrary and that distinguishing what's real from what isn't is key to my happiness. It reminds me what courage truly means.

To be afraid of something and realize it's not enough of a reason to avoid it.

Ground Rules

Me: *I want to have a productive day. There is so much I want to do!*

My thoughts: *You need to get some rest. Why don't we get mint chocolate chip ice cream and watch many many episodes of House of Cards?*

Me: *I want to write every day. It's good discipline and practice is the only way to get good at something.*

My thoughts: *You have so much to do today. Take a day off writing. It won't make a difference, and no one will know.*

Me: *I want to be healthy. I want to be fit.*

My thoughts: *Let's eat French fries and salty crunchy things and skip the gym and lounge.*

Your thoughts are fickle. They can decide to convince you of one thing (*Don't call him back! Not ever! He hurt you!*) and then decide the exact opposite (*But you love him! Love is so important! Call him now!*).

Your thoughts will toss you back and forth in a perpetual series of contradictory decisions that all sound like an excellent idea.

Better for the thinker of these thoughts to lay down some ground rules.

Good People/Bad People

Good and bad don't come in separate copper pipes like brand new plumbing.

They come in the most intricate, unexpected swirls and splotches.

There can be thirst for power in an act of generosity, despair in deception, shame in altruism, ambition in revenge, even drive within resignation.

While there can be an absolute, crystal purity in some things, such as fear, good and bad seldom arrive distilled.

Setting aside inherent contamination, the primal beast we harbor within, our basest appetites and the fact that even the best people do terrible things, I choose to believe most of us are good.

My wish for you—for everyone—is that you choose to believe this too.

Love At First Sight

I am an expert at love at first sight. It used to happen to me all the time.

I desperately loved love.

There he was, a blank canvas for everything I could possibly want him to be.

Love at first sight goes beyond liking someone for their looks because what you fall in love with doesn't come from what you see or know about the other person.

Love at first sight comes from inside of you.

You don't really know the person, which means that what you think you are seeing is not real.

What you are feeling is a mirage. It's an optical illusion conceived by yearning; a fantasy. You have all these ideas of what another should be and find a stand-in, a mirror for what you think you want reflected back to you.

You are falling in love with a character of your own fabrication, after which you are likely to disappoint yourself.

This is why it's so risky to say "I love you" too early. Because the person that you fervently declare your love to wants to make sure you are in love with who they really are and not something you have inadvertently created in your mind.

This is also why it's so common to quickly fall insanely in love only to come to your senses as you discover the other person has the audacity to be who they actually are.

No one can live up to the expectations of an overactive imagination. Even if the person was better than what you concocted you'd be too busy being disillusioned to notice.

I am not saying love at first sight is impossible. I'm saying a projection of what you want is a lot more likely.

Lest you think this reveals me as un-romantic let me tell you it's just the opposite. Love is the best thing in the world if it's real. It exceeds any fantasy.

Don't Slap A Child

I come from a time and place where slapping a child was customary. It was not considered abusive.

But it is.

You are big and she is small. She depends on you for survival. She understands the world as you define it.

You slap her and she, made of air, not yet substantial, durable, deflates until she disappears.

You disorient her. Protector, or aggressor? Should she trust you, or fear you?

You subtract admiration and awe and wonder and replace it with anger.

Slapping a child does not result in discipline. It results in internal disarray. The lesson is that she is never safe and that love comes tangled in violence.

Never slap a child.

Why Breakups Hurt

I had a room once.

It was beautiful; spacious, with high ceilings.

But as all things do, it needed a bit of work.

The floors were wood. They were scratched, dented, needed maintenance and attention to return to their original glossy color.

This is when I saw the carpet. It was stunning, multicolored, with a sheen I knew made it unique. I wanted this carpet in the room. I wanted it right away.

I don't really need to fix the floor, I decided. The carpet would cover it all.

I built the rest of the room on top of the carpet. A coffee table, a bookcase I slowly filled, a comfortable sofa. A blanket, a few pillows.

And suddenly—or maybe not so suddenly, maybe I knew this all along—the carpet was pulled out from under everything.

The table I used to put my feet on at the end of a long day, the books with the stories about the ocean. The sofa I dreamed of coming home to. And the pillows, buried under the ruins of what used to be my life.

And the floor. What did I do? Why did I think it would be a good idea to just cover it? In this time it only worsened due to lack of attention. My floor, neglected for so long, dilapidated.

I need to tear it up and begin again.

This is why breakups hurt. I loved him, for sure, but besides his loss he left behind all the things I never bothered to address in myself.

The next time I see a carpet, I'll make sure the floor I set it on has been properly, lovingly maintained. I will continue to take care of it no matter what.

Not because I believe it will one day be pulled out from under everything again, I but because I can't cover things and hope no one will know.

I will know.

Truth And Fact

Facts are the pieces of a large puzzle.

As they click into place they reveal a final image.

The final image is the truth.

Except the puzzle pieces of life are often designed to fit perfectly in more than one way.

We are each convinced that the image we see is the only one to result from the correct assembly of the puzzle pieces.

This is not always the case.

Loyalty, Misguided

If I had a boyfriend and he decided I was a mistake and my friends remained friends with him I would be so mad.

I'd want them all to take my side and not be his friends.

I mean, whatever happened to loyalty?

You know what? What I feel is always right. My feelings are what I feel and I can't control them. As such I regard them without judgement.

Now, can I actually demand that others act a certain way because of my feelings?

Can I call for my friends to stop seeing my ex-boyfriend?

I cannot.

While my feelings are never wrong this does not imply they can dictate the behavior of another person.

In fact, they don't even get to dictate my own behavior.

You can have a feeling and just hold it. Look at it. Regard it with compassion. Articulate it.

Wow, I am so angry and hurt. I feel betrayed by my friends.

You can even name it to another person.

I am angry at you for remaining friends with my ex but my feelings are my own and I will work through them. I just wanted you to know why I am acting mad and distant. Please give me a few days to sort myself out.

And then you find the power in separating what you feel from who you are.

You make a distinction between feeling something and reacting to it.

I don't know about you, but reacting to everything I was feeling was exhausting me.

I carry storms inside and learn every day how to tame my tempestuous internal weather.

So Curvy

Due to complex circumstances entirely beyond my control I have put on a bit of weight.

OK. I have put on a bit of weight because I have been eating like a frenzied beast.

Sigh.

I don't believe in diets but feel that I need to reevaluate the food choices I have been making.

Maybe I can visit the cookie place near my house twice a week instead of every day.

If someone told me six months ago *"Whoa! You look so curvy in that dress!"* I would have beamed and said *"Thank you!"*

If someone said the very same thing to me today, the frenzied beast in me might snarl.

This is why compliments need to be as clear and unambiguous as possible.

Half of the compliment resides in your intent, but the other half of what the other person hears depends on where they are at and has nothing to do with you.

Hold The Mirror

Have you ever tried to get a good look of your own back in a mirror?

You can turn, crane your neck, but you can't really see unless someone comes along with another full length mirror and holds it for you.

There you are.

This is what any relationship does for you. It holds a mirror up at certain angle, making more evident parts you would not otherwise be aware of.

This also applies to a relationship with yourself.

Looking In The Right Place

When I was 17 I went to so many big parties I didn't want to go to. So many crowded, noisy bars.

When instead I started attending things that interested me, even when I didn't meet anyone I felt more peaceful and happier.

Being alone began to feel so much better.

I learned that if I do things I don't like doing to meet people, the people I meet will like doing what I don't like to do.

If I don't like drinking (and I don't) the people I am looking for cannot be found at a bar.

If I do things I like I'll meet people like me who like me just the way I am.

Who Holds The Power In Your Relationship?

Here is what a relationship means to me.

I am happy. I would like to share this happiness with you.

The world is a big place and can be perplexing. I like your perspective and hope we can be navigation accomplices.

Let's stick together through storms and choppy waters.

I know you don't need me, and I don't need you. But it sure is awesome having you around.

To me, if at any point in the description of a relationship the notion of "power" is brought up, it would be the equivalent of opening a box of checkers and finding inside it a chess piece.

It does not belong.

If in my relationship I gave any thought at all to who had more or less power, I would reconsider its entire construction, disassemble it brick by brick and begin again.

Other Things I Recommend

I recommend a visit with an old friend you have lost touch with.

I recommend meeting someone new.

I recommend looking at the moon.

I recommend fresh flowers.

A movie on a big screen, in a movie house, with popcorn.

I recommend poetry.

I recommend chaos if you are neat and order if you are chaotic. Just for a few days.

I recommend adopting a rescued dog.

Notice something incredible, like a praying mantis or a planet.

I recommend an aquarium.

I recommend walking along a body of water—the ocean or a lake.

I recommend going to bed early.

How To Be Asked Out

If I could give my younger self advice on how to be asked out, here is what I would tell me.

Ask him out.

This will save you from games and the futility of decoding signals that might or might not exist and questions that will take up too much of your time for years.

Will he ask? Is he interested? He said he'd call me but he hasn't. What does that mean?

Don't wait for things that you want to see happen. Make them happen instead.

When you ask him out he might say no. This is the very definition of "putting yourself out there" and yes, it will hurt.

But it will also free you from waiting for something that would have never happened.

If a guy prefers it when you play hard to get, your method eliminates anyone who likes playing games.

Clean. Direct. Healthy. Set the tone for the kind of relationship you want to have.

Open

Imagine that you have a secret code and you don't want anybody to know.

Where would you keep it?

Any good hacker will tell you that no matter what you do you can't really protect a secret.

Nothing is impenetrable.

What if instead of locking it up somewhere you opened every door?

What if instead of safeguarding it you gave it away; open source?

I know this is really hard to hold but being completely vulnerable is the only way to be absolutely safe.

Emotionally Dependent/In Love

Dependency is clinging, controlling, grasping, suspicious, desperate, manipulative, needy and dramatic.

It is insatiable.

It hurts.

It is not sustainable.

I can't live without you. I will die if you leave me. I want to be with you all the time.

I don't want you to spend time with anyone other than me.

Love is clear, open, certain, serene, giving, generous, trusting, and wants whatever is best for the beloved.

I see you.

Dependency strangles love.

How To Keep The People That You Love

Boyfriend could build a tall brick tower with no windows and no doors and keep me locked inside.

I love him now but if I was kept prisoner in a tower such as this I would sit there all day dreaming of how to escape.

My longing for freedom would be so strong it would overpower any love.

Keeping me in this maximum security tower would accomplish the opposite of what he intended.

He could blindfold me so I would never look at another man and fit me with gloves so I'd never touch another and shackle me so I'd never leave him.

All of these things would accomplish the same result: despite loving him once I would want to get as far away from him as possible.

There is only one thing Boyfriend can do, which is to believe in himself and in us.

He'd then release me from this tower and open the shackles and remove the gloves and untie the blindfolds.

I'd walk free and notice other men and even feel attracted to them. But even wanting another would not threaten my relationship with him.

The only thing you can do to keep the people that you love is to be open and vulnerable and trust that you are worth loving.

Don't Be A Thief

When I look back on my life I realize that everything I have ever learned I learned from my mistakes.

Anything that I know about being capable, about being strong, about being compassionate, about being useful, and about being happy I learned from messing things up.

I want so much to save the people I love from all suffering.

But if I did that successfully I would rob them of everything.

Lose Yourself/Find Yourself

Let's say I meet a guy.

I like him a lot so I pretend to like what he likes.

I want decisions to be easy so I go along with whatever he wants to do.

Soon I can't tell if I like something or "we" like something.

This is how I delude myself into thinking I have lost myself.

The truth is I don't actually lose myself (although it feels that way). I am still here, making my voice heard in unsuspecting ways.

I get angry at small things, feel irritable and impatient.

I begin to speak up. It's a voice of dissent and this confuses the guy. All he has ever known is me agreeing with everything so I can't fault him for suddenly not recognizing me. I have never let him see me.

Speaking up feels good. It feels right. I do it in small ways first, and as my voice grows stronger I speak up in more meaningful ways.

I'm afraid, of course. Of losing his approval, of this guy deciding maybe we don't have that much in common and that he doesn't like me anymore.

But I've had enough of compromising myself and decide to push through this fear.

I'd rather not be liked by him than not be liked by me.

I don't want to go back to feeling lost, so empty and confused; not remembering what it's like to stand up for who I am.

And that's how you find yourself.

Cassandra's Curse

Humans have an astounding ability to completely disregard the most important things.

For example: we are all going to die. You know this. I know this.

But we live as if we didn't know.

Then one of us experiences something devastating, or frightening, or astonishing, and with a renewed, blinding flash of staggering insight we return from said experience with an urgent message.

We desperately want to bestow unto others what we have seen, in all its clarity and foresight.

OH MY GOD WE ARE ALL GOING TO DIE WE ARE SPENDING TIME ON THINGS THAT DON'T MATTER

And everyone nods and agrees and—

Promptly goes back to living life as if we had forever.

My favorite Greek myth is Cassandra's curse.

She was given the power of prophecy.

She could see the future, but when she told others what she saw, often with despair, with urgency, nobody believed her.

There is a little bit of Cassandra's curse in all of us.

Relationship History

We all have patterns, tend to fight over similar things with different people, reveal a lot about ourselves when we talk about others, and break up for similar reasons.

A person's past behavior is a good indicator for future behavior.

This reminds me of a scene in Sex and the City. Carrie Bradshaw meets a guy in the waiting room of her therapist's office and they end up in bed together.

After they have sex he asks her why she was seeing a therapist.

"I pick the wrong men", she says. "What about you?"

"I lose interest in a woman after I sleep with her."

Is That Really True?

Have you heard about Byron Katie?

She realized, consistent with the ancient Greeks, Zen tradition and Buddhism, that believing her own thoughts was the source of all her suffering.

She proceeded to write several best selling books based on this insight and developed a method called *The Work*.

The intent of *The Work* is for the thoughts that you are convinced are true to loosen their hold on you.

She doesn't want you convinced they are not true.

She wants you to wonder.

Here is a quick summary of *The Work:*

Identify something you are convinced of that makes you suffer.

This could be anything: I am not good enough, no one will ever love me, I am a loser.

For the purposes of this demonstration of *The Work* let's go with

"My boss thinks my work sucks."

You then ask yourself the following questions that you need to really, deeply ponder for a while, not check off in quick succession.

In other words, sit there and really search inside yourself.

Is this true? *(A typical response would sound like Oh my god yes my boss thinks everything I do is crap just this morning he glared at me and said....)*

Can I absolutely know it's true? *(Well yes I just told you this is what I believe in!)*

How do I react—what happens—when I believe this? *(It's so stressful it makes me feel sad and small and like nothing I do is ever good enough! Ack! Ack!)*

Who would I be without this thought? *(I feel...free. Peaceful.)*

Once you are done with all the questions comes the best part.

The turnaround.

Turn your thought around by considering different versions of the exact opposite.

To continue with my example, the turnarounds could be:

My boss loves me.

I think I suck.

I think my boss sucks.

Take each one of your masterfully created turnarounds and add *The Work* again. (Is this true? Is this truer?)

What happens to your brain when you do this and sleep on it is the most fascinating part.

The work done diligently implants in your mind new possibilities, other alternatives to things that cause you anxiety, and sets you free.

Please Love Me, Please Leave Me

We all have an insistent, primal voice in our head that, in an effort to protect us, constantly whispers two urgent, desperate things:

You are in danger.

You don't have enough.

Sometimes this voice speaks the truth but most of the time it's on overdrive.

Its job is to constantly freak out.

My job is to get a handle on my insecurities.

If I listen to this voice and let it overtake other more reasonable voices inside my head I will be under the delusion that I am never safe and that everything is scarce and will require constant, insatiable proof that things are not in a state of irreparable crisis.

If someone loves me, I feel compelled to test that love.

Pushing people away is a common way to do this: if I push you away and you stay that might mean I am on solid ground, at least until the next time I am convinced I am in danger or need another hit of that delicious rush of feeling that I am on solid ground. (A few seconds from now. No, wait. Now.)

If I was in love with someone who repeatedly asked me to leave I would say *"If you are testing my love I want you to know I love you and don't want to leave. But you should also know that I too deserve to feel safe so if you ask me again to leave I will do so and not look back. Please carefully consider what you are asking me to do."*

I would not say this in the spirit of a threat. I'd keep my word.

Our feeling fleetingly safe cannot come at the cost of causing pain and distress to the person we love.

The next time you are in the throes of your own insecurities remember this: love does not conquer all.

Insecurity annihilates love.

The Wrong Filter

I have two captivating, handsome, talented friends.

They both work in jobs where they interact with a lot of people.

One, let's call him Moe, is loving, receptive and open. He spends time with his team, is dedicated to his work and makes it a point to mentor others.

Joe is guarded. People ask to spend time with him and he declines, not to carve time for himself but because he'd rather not get attached.

Moe, approachable, vulnerable, attracts loving relationships.

Those who pursue Joe do so aggressively. After he says "I can't" many become insistent.

Those who eventually push their way to getting closer to him are the very ones who disregarded his initial boundaries.

It's like he set his filter wrong.

Joe repeatedly attracts tumultuous, stormy relationships that leave him feeling like he would rather not get attached.

The dynamic begins again.

Is it this simple? Could there be more to what I see unfold before me?

I'm sure there is.

But it has shown me that the mechanisms we put in place to protect ourselves don't always work the way we expect; and that the stories in our life that repeat themselves—all those things that happen to us again and again—yield important information essential to our happiness.

It is self-awareness that keeps us safe, much more than shutting down love or closing ourselves off to others.

Alone

A few weeks ago I experienced a severe episode of vertigo. I was sitting on the couch and the world started spinning. The sensation was so bad I couldn't even sit up, much less stand.

Boyfriend was with me and dragged me to the bathroom so I could throw up.

He called into work to say he wasn't coming in so he could stay with me.

He remained close all day, attempted to hold me, placed cold compresses on the back of my neck and tried—mostly in vain—to feed me.

My recurring thought through all of this was *"Oh my god. I wish he could, but he can't help me."*

Him embracing me did not stop the world from moving. He was a mensch and yet nothing he did could make me feel better.

I appreciated his company and support but this was my battle and I needed to get through it on my own.

It's easier to understand this when the symptoms are physical but the same applies to our mental state.

Our battles happen in a place no one can reach and although we can be supported and kept company, in a very real sense we wage them alone.

Does The Universe Conspire In My Favor?

Let's say I love writing.

I would write if I had the time. But, my house is not going to clean itself. And I have to go to work. Writing seldom pays the bills.

So my writing muscles lie there, unattended and indolent.

One day I decide I have to write.

I vow to do so every single day, long or short, good or bad.

At first I wonder what to write about.

To keep my vow my writing antenna are always up. I prowl, voracious, eyes open, ears open, mind open, eager for material.

Stories begin to appear everywhere. In conversations I overhear, in my own thoughts and memories, in my friends and their dynamics, in my family and my relationships.

I cannot get through a single hour without taking notes of something.

What happened?

Did the whole universe conspire to lovingly present stories to me like sacred offerings so that I could write?

It sure feels that way. But it did not.

The stories were there all along.

What changed was what I very deliberately decided to focus on.

This is the power of your own attention.

Playing It Safe/Being A Coward

How does what you do make you feel?

Playing it safe to me would feel prudent, judicious, discerning, reasonable, responsible, even shrewd.

If I wanted to do something and I didn't because I was afraid, being discerning would give way to feeling tight, apprehensive, meek.

Playing it safe doesn't feel timorous. It feels solid.

Failing to act because of fear doesn't feel firm. It feels like I'm shrinking.

Only You

I am in an advanced yoga class.

My level really depends on the day.

"Yogis, please come down to Hanumanasana."

The teacher says *"You are warmed up so this is the best time to try this pose!"*

Many of my friends are in it.

Strangers around me are in it.

My ego is, as usual, hyper and enthusiastic *YES WE CAN DO THIS IT WILL BE GLORIOUS WE WILL BE IMPRESSIVE!*

I really want to do what everyone is doing and am considering my options.

That's when I hear her, firm and clear.

My inner voice.

Dushka. Some day. Not today.

You can adjust this pose to your ability. You can even stretch, push yourself, find your edge. But don't risk injury.

This pose, at least for now, is not for you.

No matter what is happening around you, only you can decide what works for you.

Not your loved ones. Not your teachers. Not your friends. Not strangers. Not "everybody".

Online Dating—Off To A Good Start

When I dated online, this is what stood out to me:

A man who wrote well, used complete sentences and knew where to put his apostrophes.

A tone that was direct and above playing games.

A thoughtful note that referenced something in my profile. *"I would love to meet you because I too find walking in the rain completely overrated."*

A guy who would reach out with the intent to meet, rather than an intent to be a pen pal.

Someone with a specific plan in mind that showed they had spent a bit of time thinking about what to do. *"You mentioned you liked tea and I know a great tea place."*

Extra points if the date was simple, yet showed a bit of imagination. *"There is a bookstore right next to the tea place—maybe afterwards we can go see if we find something worth recommending to each other."*

"Even if the date doesn't work out, we both end up with a book we wouldn't have otherwise chosen" for me pretty much closes the deal.

Meditation

Meditation will change your life.

If you give it a chance you will feel calmer, more focused and happier.

Meditation makes you emotionally stronger because instead of getting "hooked into" the feelings that you experience, you recognize them as something separate from who you are.

It's harder for them to take you on that wild, unsustainable, exhausting roller coaster ride.

What you need to do to be an accomplished meditator is to focus on your breath.

That's it.

Do it every day, even if you only focus on your breath for a couple of minutes.

Pick a quiet spot and time of day. You can, for example, wake up a bit earlier than everyone else.

Or, pick any time of day and hide in the bathroom.

You need to be, just for a snippet of time you lovingly give yourself, free of external distractions.

Make sure you sit in a position where your spine is straight.

Your mind will do what minds do. It will think. It will wander. It will produce list after list of things to do, things you need to get at the supermarket, things you have forgotten, things you better not have forgotten, a list of more important things to do than sit there and do nothing.

It will tell you that it's much more important to be busy.

It will make your nose itch.

It will tell you you are sooooo soooo sleeeeepy.

It will tell you to be very concerned that you are "not doing it right."

It will get you to freak out.

Allow all this to happen. Regard it without judgement. *"Huh. Look! All the things Dushka said!"*

Ignore everything, let it pass you by, and focus on your breath.

Misnomer

The term "comfort zone" sounds comfortable, but instead it's where nothing exciting or new ever happens.

It's back there where you never take risks, never feel thrilled, never feel nervous, never feel elated, never surprise yourself by doing something you didn't think you could do.

That comfort zone is where your senses get dulled, when you don't notice anything around you, not even beautiful things, because if you see something every day even beauty becomes tiring.

Your comfort zone is every single day feeling like Wednesday, food tasting like what you had yesterday and the day before.

It imperceptibly becomes low grade despair.

Never leaving your comfort zone extinguishes your curiosity, your creativity, your sense of purpose and your drive.

You can switch it all off and live on automatic and wonder what it's all for and many other things it doesn't occur to you to wonder if you are even sometimes on your toes.

Happiness hides in a thousand unexpected places but your comfort zone is not one of them.

Not even contentment likes that dreary place.

Save Yourself Some Time

Don't play hard to get.

In fact, don't play at all.

Don't try to read into hints or try to hint at something someone else has to try to read.

Don't ask a friend to ask a friend if he likes you. Don't tell a friend to tell a friend you like him.

Don't wonder what something means or get together with friends to try to figure out what that certain inflection could possibly imply.

Don't try to think hard about someone in the hopes they will feel you thinking.

Don't introduce any form of uncertainty into anything you want for sure.

Instead, walk up to the person you want to get to know/miss/kiss/snuggle/canoodle/be friends with and state your case.

State it clear and state it strong because regardless of how the other person reacts, regardless of the games the other person might or might not counter with, clear and strong is what you should always be.

Empathy/Compassion

Compassion (very much like gratitude) is a game changer.

Instead of going through each day in the roller coaster that is reacting to everything (I'm angry! I'm annoyed! I'm irritated! I'm insulted!), with compassion my life can be more centered and peaceful.

Empathy means understanding how others feel; putting yourself in the shoes of another person.

Compassion adds love to this understanding.

In its purest form it really means feeling love for all beings, even our enemies.

Yes. Of course I find this as mind-bending as you do.

But, think about traffic and how exhausting it can be to sit there seething because everyone is insulting you, threatening you, attacking you, disrespecting you.

What if I could sit there full of love for everyone instead? What would that do to me and my well-being?

How much better would it be to take all the anger coursing inside me and replace it with grace?

I want that.

Lucky for me (and for you) compassion—like gratitude, like meditation, like deep breathing—is a practice.

It's a habit anyone can pick up.

The next time I feel *aaaaaaaarrrrgg* towards someone, I will try to see if I can feel compassion.

I will start with myself.

You are so ack why did you eat that delectable cookie when you said you wanted to be healthier

I notice the absence of compassion towards myself.

I note that they are just thoughts and that I can replace them with positive thoughts *I have done so many smart things so many times I have triumphed that delectable cookie was so delicious I love myself it will be ok* and feel so much better.

Compassion feels better than hate. From practicing compassion towards myself I move on (noting the aggressive thought—replacing it with a positive thought) to the people that I love, and then slowly, very slowly to the people that I don't.

Loving all beings is not something I came up with. It's a Buddhist tradition available to everyone.

Metta Bhavana is a loving kindness meditation about cultivating love for all beings; wishing all beings freedom and happiness.

It's as difficult for me as it is for you and it changes everything.

Never Stop Learning

The instant you stop learning your life is suddenly behind you.

Ask a stranger in a bookstore to recommend a book.

Go watch a movie you normally would not be interested in. I like children's movies. Kids laugh in completely different places and I walk out of the theater bewildered and joyfully off-balance.

Take time off work to go to a late afternoon workshop on something that unexpectedly peaked your curiosity. Ikebana, modern architecture, poisonous plants.

Try learning a new language and marvel at how similar and different it is from your own, how much it reveals about the people who speak it. In English you "kill two birds with one stone." In Italian you "feed two birds with one bean."

Talk to someone from your childhood about all you remember. Learn how treacherous memory is, how slippery, how you have completely different recollections of identical incidents.

Question what you think you know. Learn to celebrate chaos, lack of meaning and uncertainty. But whatever you do, never stop learning.

Thank You, Quora

A condition to writing is shutting everything else out.

You go at it alone, and as such it can be isolating.

You create your own world and circumscribe yourself to it.

It never occurred to me that instead of secluding me it could connect me.

I never considered it would somehow lead to engagement.

How impossibly beautiful.

When I came across Quora, the question and answer format lent itself to sharing with others anything I had ever found that made things easier.

I find life to be both simple and tricky, like a puzzle. Solving something or seeing things in a way that contributed to me suffering less could perhaps prove useful to others.

The messages I receive on Quora have given my writing a new dimension.

Readers tell me that I contribute to their lives, that I have an impact on their perspective.

This has caused an internal shift that I find eye opening, motivating and inspiring.

A virtuous circle.

I inspire you with something that worked for me, you for me open up my formerly circumscribed world.

I hear often that social media "doesn't matter." What does it all mean, anyway? What the heck is an "upvote?" What is Quora and who cares if you have "followers?"

If social media is used to measure your life against others or as a way to amass "friends" who really aren't then I guess the fact that it means nothing is true.

But if it allows you to make useful something you do for love, if through sharing something you can make another person's life more palatable, if someone comes across something I write and feels like it was what they were looking for or what they needed, I can't think of anything with more meaning than that.

Baby Dragons

Back when I was first assembled someone left behind a tangle of strong, young, wild feelings in perpetual disarray.

I imagine them like a litter of baby dragons, hungry and curious and tripping over their big, clawed feet.

My task was to keep them from going feral.

Most of the time I am under the illusion I have partially domesticated them.

Look at them, curled up and placid.

But then something ignites them and they unfurl, gigantic, unmanageable, unbridled, abrupt.

Breathing is the only thing I have found that keeps them separate from me.

"WHOA LET'S ALL TAKE A BREATH." I can say.

"Maybe we don't all have to be instantly irritated or angry or defensive."

This partition is all it takes for me to see I am not my anxiety, or my jealousy or my impetuousness.

I am not my worry, my wrath, my disappointment, my pain.

I am not my hunger, my desire, my lust.

These now adolescent beasts don't get to command immediate reactions from me.

This distinction makes all the difference.

Trust Your Feet

My 8 year old niece is taking rock climbing lessons.

I wish I had her teacher coach me through life.

Here are some notes from the class:

The only way is up.

Trust your feet.

Use all your limbs.

Focus.

Keep moving up.

You are safe.

Use your legs the most so you don't burn out.

Don't burn out.

Use everything.

Move with your breath.

Rock your weight. Distribute your strength.

Protect yourself. Clip that rope in.

I know you want to take a step down. Fight that.

Don't get off course.

Get around that.

You know how to get there.

You are safe.

Focus.

Don't rush it. Look at the path and figure out what you are going to do.

You've got the moves. It's just that the cliff looks scary but you have to trust yourself.

Use all your toes.

Bring your feet with you.

Focus.

It feels like you are not doing well but look how far the floor is.

Use everything.

We should all take rock climbing lessons.

Comparing Myself To Others

The first time I went to a yoga class I did not want to go back.

Everyone was better than me.

Everyone was bendier and more graceful. I couldn't even touch my toes.

The more I looked at others the worse I did.

Not only because I felt increasingly inadequate but because I forced myself into the poses they could do and I couldn't.

Ouch.

I found that if I focused on myself I made a lot more progress.

I had to begin by accepting exactly where I was.

I had to determine what worked for me, regardless of what worked for everyone else.

I stopped comparing myself to others when I understood that every second spent looking at someone else would be better spent working on myself.

Unlikely Skill

Before the existence of computers, before the Internet, we used pencils and notebooks to write, and we used typewriters.

While using a typewriter was not considered necessary, I believed that the ability to quickly bang out a perfectly legible document on one would be pretty rad.

So I took lessons.

I learned how to type by resting all my fingers on the keys and writing page after page of exercises like *ffff jjjj* or *aaaa qqqq* or *llll mmmm*.

I learned to type sentences that contained every letter such as *pack my box with five dozen jugs of liquid veneer.*

I had no way of knowing that some day far into the future I would spend most of the day typing on a not yet invented device currently known as keyboard.

Today I type like a beast. I use all my fingers.

I can type blindfolded.

My fingers can type one document while I glance at another.

I guess that in some worlds all this is super geeky but in my world (that I alone inhabit) it's insanely cool.

The best thing you can do today is identify an unlikely skill that intrigues you and learn as much about it as you can.

It doesn't matter if it doesn't make sense.

It doesn't matter if everyone thinks it's boring.

It doesn't matter if all evidence points to the fact you will probably never put it to good use.

Because at worst learning more about anything that interests you is a wonderful way to go through life.

And at best you might become dexterous at a skill that will prove indispensable to your future self.

Beautiful

I can't tell you how many times I am with a person I love (friend, family member, significant other, even co-worker) and we are chatting or laughing or in the middle of something and suddenly I am stunned by their beauty.

It's easy to take in an external harmony of features and confuse it with beauty but real beauty is more like an inner radiance and it takes your breath away.

One fine day you will look at someone you love and understand what I am trying to tell you.

It doesn't matter what you look like.

You are beautiful.

Be A Baby

Have you ever seen a baby learn to walk?

She wobbles up knowing full well she will fall.

She doesn't care about looking like a fool, failing over and over, or rolling on her side belly up.

She doesn't ask for the secret formula to go from sitting to standing.

She doesn't line up everything to make sure it all goes perfectly.

The endeavor is messy, noisy, sloppy, spirited and stubborn. She pushes up and goes, falls down, gets up again and again and again until her first steps are taken.

She wants to get from here to there. She doesn't become fixated on how—she becomes fixated with wanting to get from here to there.

This will do.

What she's trying to accomplish is tectonic. She can't even see it. But think about it: today, the coffee table. Tomorrow, the Appalachian Trail.

By this I mean you have no way of knowing just how far you will go.

For now it just matters that you begin.

Be a baby.

Do Me

If Boyfriend looked me over salaciously and said he'd do me I'd consider it flattering. (I mean, I already know, but please tell me more.)

If a friend came over to pick me up looking gorgeous and I said *"Whoa! You look amazing! I'd totally do you!"* we'd both laugh hysterically.

Saying this to a friend would be mildly out of place and a tad out of character which is what would make it funny. (In fact, I will try this tonight at dinner with friends.)

If a stranger came up to me in a bar and said *"I'd do you"* I'd consider it crude. I prefer wit and a bit more imagination.

In some cultures, such as Mexico (where I'm from) if a guy came over to my house and said *"I'd do her"* referring to my sister or my mother that would be very insulting.

What makes an expression offensive is not the expression alone but the intent and context, which applies to nearly any expression.

How To Be An Optimist

I was blessed with a natural predisposition towards optimism.

Without making any less of my good fortune I do work very hard to wrangle wayward, rebellious, dark thoughts into bow and rainbow shapes.

If my perspective can diminish pain I say yes, please. How do I need to look at this so that I suffer less?

I have two "go to" ways to get myself out of a funk in moments of despair. (They work if I can remember them.)

Say something makes me angry or frustrated. My insides rage. I hear a thousand indignant voices in the middle of which I try to slip in a question.

What is this here to teach me?

The notion that something was sent to me lovingly to be a teacher rather than an aggressor alters the angle that traps me so I can wriggle free.

As an added bonus occasionally I also learn something.

If you need to stand in line for two hours at the DMV, Dushka, I tell myself, *maybe you need to learn a bit of patience.*

The second "go to" method that tends to work has to do with getting out of my own head.

The situation you are in totally sucks but there are other people in the world besides you. Anything you could be doing to make someone else's life a bit better?

If bad things have to happen we might as well make ourselves useful.

The Crook Of My Arm

When I dated online I spent loads of time closely studying profiles.

I wanted to make sure I had good experiences; met people I liked and found interesting.

The extra time spent reading the information offered reduced the chances I'd have a bad date.

Plus, they were fascinating and revealed so much.

I came across a compelling, well written profile of a guy who declared his pet peeve was women who carried their purse on the crook of their elbow.

For reasons unrelated to this comment I never reached out to him.

We did not meet, interact or exchange a single note.

To put it in other words, he was not important to me.

It's been years since I read that and I always remember him when I rest the handles of my purse on the crook of my elbow.

I think about this a lot.

Somehow not wanting to fall into the "pet peeve" category of an utter stranger got etched into my brain.

This is in part because we are wired to amass approval—the more people like us the better our chances of survival.

Getting others to like us has the power to mold the things we do and who we become.

The trick is to let this contribute to our growth, to make us better without allowing it to compromise who we are.

This requires vigilance over why we do what we do.

I will carry my purse in whatever way I find most comfortable.

How To Change Your Outlook

Do what you need to do to come at things with an optimistic attitude. You can't hear opportunity knocking if you are convinced opportunity never does.

Acknowledge you have more power than you think. This might or might not be true, but the acknowledgment changes what you are able to perceive.

If you ever feel you have no choice make a list of choices. Get friends to help. Throw a choice party. Prove to your brain there is no such thing as "I have no choice."

Assume you know nothing. It's not that you are ignorant. It's that knowing nothing implies a whole world of possibilities available to you right around the corner.

Believe fervently in serendipity. Believe in sheer good fortune. Believe others want to help. Otherwise you will miss perfectly good offerings you are not receptive to.

Don't believe your own thoughts. Your brain is wired to make you afraid. It thinks it's the most likely way for you to survive. This strategy is not necessary. At least not all of the time.

Just because someone tells you a certain solution has not worked for anyone doesn't mean it can't work for you.

Get enough sleep. Sleep deprivation makes you delusional.

Search for silence every day.

Talk to a friend every day.

Help someone else out every day.

Exercise every day.

Honor what you feel. "This totally sucks and I am sad" is valid and fair and often true.

Be grateful every day. This points out what you have rather than what you don't.

Treasure Hunt

Imagine if you will that you are about to participate in a thrilling treasure hunt.

You get no instruction manual. No book of rules. No clear sense of what you are supposed to do or how to get to the finish line.

You don't know what the finish line is.

You might feel tempted to look around and do what others are doing but soon catch on to the fact that everyone is winging it.

You can go at this treasure hunt alone, or you can pick an accomplice.

You get to choose what characteristics this accomplice of yours should have.

He might have skills that are complimentary to yours, be better than you at distinguishing vision from delusion, at making out the lighthouse through the thick fog.

There will often be thick fog.

Maybe walking next to this person just makes the largely nonsensical treasure hunt more *fun*.

Maybe he has a way of opening your mind, interpreting things differently.

Maybe he points out things to notice along the way you might not have noticed on your own.

There is a lot to be said for being fascinated.

As you can probably tell, it's wonderful if your partner in crime is attractive but it might not necessarily be high on the list of priorities given all the other crucial things to consider.

More to the point, in the middle of turbulence and adventure he will have your back and you will have his.

No matter what you look like to others you will look gorgeous to each other.

We Create What Destroys Us

I have a friend who is perpetually overwhelmed.

She quit from a job because she "had no work life balance" and is having the same problem in her new job.

"Everyone wants a piece of me, Dushka" she says. *"I am at the end of my rope."*

"How would you feel if no one in the world needed you?" I ask. *"If your phone never rang, if your inbox was always empty?"*

She looks crestfallen.

"Oh my God. I would feel horrible."

The realization that we often create the things that end up destroying us, the things that hinder us from being happy, is the first step to setting down what burdens us.

Why Life Is Not A Movie

In the movies, it's when everything is perfect and everybody is happy that you know something disastrous is about to happen.

The car skids. The child wanders off into the woods. Smoke billows.

Well, life is not a movie.

Wonderful things will keep happening to me, one after the other, in obscene excess.

The other shoe is not going to drop.

There is no limit to how happy I can be, and this also holds true for you.

Life-Long Exercise

Let's pretend I have a dark secret.

I believe I am not good enough and therefore I operate under that assumption.

I am convinced that in order to deserve love I have to please others.

I have to work at getting people to like me.

If someone else wants anything from me I am compelled to provide it. Otherwise, they won't want to be with me.

Examples of what other people might want from me vary broadly: help with their homework, keeping their secrets, liking what they like, wanting to do what they want to do. Sex.

I'm almost pleading at first. I jump at the chance to give what I can.

But then, wait a minute. This isn't right.

I feel used, become resentful, angry.

Resentment is a symptom of poor boundaries. I shouldn't have let it get this far.

Another symptom of poor boundaries is the sense something is wrong with "everybody."

Why is everybody using me? Why does everyone lie to me? Why does everyone end up betraying me?

Boundaries are hard to set—saying no is difficult—because the underlying belief is that saying no will cost me the relationship. It is an indication that I am not giving enough, that I am not loyal enough, not dedicated enough.

It must mean I'm selfish.

But setting boundaries is not selfish. It's healthy. It's how I respect myself.

Look around you. Boundaries are why fences exist, and walls and doors and curtains. They are indispensable for our well-being.

I need to honor myself enough to acknowledge that my boundaries can and will shift. They are mine, so they can do anything they want.

Yesterday I was happy to help you with your homework. I am not willing to do it today. I had sex with you last night. I don't want to this morning. I don't have to explain.

Boundary setting is a life-long exercise that you often need to re-examine, re-establish. I am giving up my weekend to finish what my boss asked me to do. I'm working late, again.

I'm saying yes when I want to say no to get someone to think well of me.

I need to be brave enough to say: this is who I am. This is what I like. This is what I can do for you. But, you can't push against who I am. You can't get me to like something I don't.

You can't get me to do anything that makes me uncomfortable.

My discomfort for your benefit is not healthy for either of us.

Needed

We all need so much to feel needed and yet refuse to ask for help.

Asking for help makes us vulnerable, and it makes us feel we are putting a burden on another.

If you refuse to ask for help, you rob another person of the joy of feeling needed.

Give them that.

Leap Of Faith

To me, a leap of faith has to do with believing in something within you.

Every worthwhile quest or pursuit—such as the pursuit of happiness—sooner or later requires a leap of faith (or many).

A moment where you know with certainty something that for others seems implausible.

"This makes no sense" everyone you know says.

"This makes no sense" your brain says.

"But, I have to" your gut replies.

Your gut is glorious.

Rainbow

A couple of years ago I was walking along an empty road and looked up to see an insane, bright double rainbow.

I stood there, slack-jawed.

Ooooh.

"Look!" I told Boyfriend. *"Fill your eyes with that!"*

Ooooooooh.

I was so happy I had someone to share that rainbow with. I would have been perfectly OK gawking at it alone but being able to thwack someone else's shoulder and point made it extra special.

You love not because you need someone.

Not because the other might some day prove useful.

You love because love is awesome.

Because in the company of the right person there is no telling what you can become.

Relationships are for walking with someone along sometimes rocky, sometimes rainbow lit roads.

Should You Push Yourself To Write?

I don't like the word "push."

Whenever I feel pushed I don't react well. Pushing me is not the way to get me to do anything. Not even when I'm pushing myself.

What if you instead make some space? Imagine a circle around you that belongs to you alone. Sit in the middle and write.

How about if instead you coaxed? Use your sweetest voice, set out cookies. Pull out a chair and write.

Have you tried cajoling? Teasing? Flirting? Seducing? Enticing?

Pushing can be counterproductive.

Try more alluring things and write.

How To Get Over Being Cheated On

I'm going to tell you something about infidelity that is very difficult to understand and that at first you might even find insulting.

Ready?

It's not personal.

I know that sounds preposterous. I know it feels so intensely personal and in your face and up in your business and it fucks you up, right?

Right?

But hear me out.

Being cheated on hurts for many reasons but in part screams right in your ear your biggest fear.

You are not enough, and someone else is better.

But, that's just not true.

Instead, this has nothing to do with you and your awesomeness.

Fabulous, wonderful people get cheated on.

The person who cheated could have handled things differently and instead decided to lie. To double cross. To do something despite knowing it would hurt a loved one.

That's an issue, and it's on the cheater. Not on you.

And that's how you begin to get over being cheated on.

How To Solve A Problem

First, I remind myself that I am only looking at this problem in one way.

I forget, but there is always a different way to see something.

My reality is not objective reality. It's just the angle with which I am regarding something.

Just because I can't see it doesn't mean there is no solution.

Second, I try to get rid of thoughts like "this can't be done" or "there is no hope" or "there is no way out."

I want my brain to know it can think as creatively as it wants, even when it comes up with ridiculous things.

Third, I embrace all the things I don't know.

Everything that I don't know brings with it the potential for ways to solve the problem that are at the moment not within my sphere of thought.

How can I look at this in another way? What am I missing?

Fourth, I force myself to make a list of the choices that I have, ten, maybe twenty choices, even if they are preposterous.

My brain needs to be reminded that when it comes to choices there will never be a shortage.

Fifth, I sleep on the problem. I come at it on a brand new day, well rested, after a good breakfast, and look at it again.

I can't guarantee that with this five step method I am able to solve any problem. In fact, many things don't get solved at all.

But I look back at what I have accomplished all those times I thought I couldn't, or that I was convinced there was no way, and can tell you I've achieved things I initially believed to be impossible.

How To Deal With Someone Better Than You

I want anyone better than me to be a part of my life. Be my boss. Work with me, for me. Be my friend, my advisor, my mentor, a member of my imaginary board of directors.

Hang out with me.

All the people in my life are better than me. You'd realize this within seconds if you met anyone in my family.

Boyfriend anchors my flights of fancy. My best friend taught me about friendship by being the best example. The people I have worked with have taught me grace and patience.

OK. I haven't learned much about patience; but I can't fault others for that.

Do I ever feel jealous or envious of their grandiosity, their talent, their steadiness? Perhaps. But I'll be darned if I let these feelings, petty, unsubstantial, come between me and my ability to learn from others.

I prefer awe.

I cannot allow my insecurities to keep me small.

Fact: You become like the people you surround yourself with.

May I forever walk among giants.

Should I Ask My Crush Why She Stares At Me?

I'm going to tell you a secret I discovered some time ago that is so simple and basic and obvious that I missed it for years.

A lot of what we get in life rests on our ability to ask the right question.

A precise, targeted question is more likely to deliver what I really want to know.

If my crush was staring at me, why he was staring would be a secondary question.

What is it that I'd really want to know?

What I would want to know is if he had a crush on me too.

Once I identified the right question, I would definitely walk over to him and say *"I like you. Do you like me too?"*

And then, I would know.

It's A System

Picture if you will a man who smokes.

He notices that the more he smokes the more he wants to.

For him smoking began as a way to pass the time, then became a habit, then a vice.

The more he did it, the stronger it became.

This is how he realized any habit becomes stronger as you feed it.

Now the man would like to stop smoking. It's an incredibly difficult habit to break.

He notices that as he tries again and again his smoking diminishes.

Now he thinks he wants to exercise more.

He perhaps begins to make healthier decisions when it comes to what he chooses to eat.

You see, every one of our habits is connected to the other.

Our habits are not isolated behavior. They are a system. All together they add up to the quality and condition of our life.

Breathing and how we do it is, in a way, the original habit.

It's the very first thing we ever did, we need to do it constantly and it regulates everything in our body and our mind.

If our breaths are quick and shallow we are signaling to our brain we are in danger.

Our brain responds with a flight or fight reaction by producing a steady stream of stress hormones, designed to be doled out in a single quick spurt to handle a specific threat.

Teaching ourselves to make our breaths deeper, longer, slower tells our brain it can relax. We shift into rest and digest mode. This reduces the stress hormones released into our system.

Breathing is important because we need it to live, but we also need it to live better.

Like the first dominoes in a long chain, breathing is intrinsically connected to everything we do.

The best part is that breathing is free and it's there for us always. When we are happy, satisfied, distressed, alone, frightened, threatened, desperate and enthusiastic.

Find your breath.

"Easy" Is A Decoy

"Hard" has somehow gotten a bad reputation.

Please don't listen to any that. It's drivel.

"Hard" is unspeakably cool. It's where the challenge is, the temerity, the audacity and the struggle.

It's where you find satisfaction and accomplishment.

It's where anything worthy gets assembled.

"Easy" has a good reputation, but it's absurdly overrated.

If you decide to do things based on the criteria that they will be easy, easy will repeatedly steer you wrong.

Don't you see? Easy is a decoy.

Believe me when I tell you this. "Hard" is where it's at.

How To Explain Divorce To A Kid

You set the tone. If you are anxious, weepy, angry, resentful, it's not a good time to talk to her. You need to transmit stability, safety, peace. Divorce is a solution. I am here to present you with something that will make our lives better, not worse.

You loving each other and never saying anything to put her down is pretty much the most important thing you can do from here on.

The two of you (the parents) need to be in lockstep about the important things. One can't give permission while the other denies permission. You can't begin to blame each other for whatever. It's confusing.

Your daughter needs to learn the importance of not settling into unhappiness. Your divorce is a lesson in the pursuit of happiness. This is an invaluable life skill, in my experience much better than growing up in a house where everyone is miserable (or near-homicidal).

Your daughter will assume this is her fault. We perceive the world through our own eyes, so she will believe she did something to cause this. You need to reassure her as often as possible that this has nothing to do with her.

Please don't lie to her. She probably already knows. This means she will believe you more than she believes herself. You don't want her to learn she cannot trust her own intuition.

Finally, be ready to provide logistical information. What you might think is "the details" is pretty much the center of her existence. Where will she sleep? Where will she keep her things? What if she is with her mom and wants you to tuck her in?

You need to be ready to answer these questions in the most honest, reassuring way you can. It's OK if you sometimes say "I don't know."

My parents getting a divorce sucked.

It was the best thing they could have done for me.

Bad At It

Let's say I want to learn how to ice skate.

I want to learn, which implies I don't know how.

If I put ice skates on and get on the ice I'm going to look ridiculous.

I will hold on to the sides of the rink, grab on to people as they swoosh past me, fall repeatedly, maybe even hurt myself.

To get to the part where I look moderately graceful on that ice I have to suck at it first.

I have to try and fail and fall and get up and try again and take risks and lift a foot and cross it over to put it in front of the other and glide for a fraction of a second and stumble and trip on myself.

If I keep going, past my fear and my concerns about my ego getting bruised (or my knees), I eventually put most of the incompetence behind me and look effortless and extend my arms out and feel the cold wind in my hair and do a half forward fold and raise a leg back and take a turn and listen to everyone tell me again and again how easy I make this look.

To be good at something, you have to be bad at it.

Please Don't Save Me

After my divorce a beloved, well intentioned friend insisted that what I needed was to sleep around. Casual sex was, according to him, what would pull me out of my state of emotional paralysis.

My friend meant well. He loves me and wanted to see me happy and was perhaps coming at the problem from his own perspective.

Meaning, if this was his problem, casual sex would do the trick.

Except that for me, this was not "a problem." I was sad and being sad honored how I felt. I was fine hanging on to feeling sad until I was good and ready.

On a related note, casual sex is not my thing. Sex makes me feel deeply attached and my emotions were already sufficiently rocked.

Only one person was going to get me from being miserable to feeling like myself, and that person was me.

This was my process, and no one could save me but myself.

I am very much in favor of supporting a loved one and being there to help.

But, you cannot "make" someone else happy.

You cannot "help" someone through addiction.

You cannot "save" another.

This is not your role.

Being a savior is dangerous. It assumes you know better. It assumes the other person is in some way helpless to do this for herself.

As such, as counterintuitive as this might sound, playing the hero is an act of ego.

The support one should provide is more receptive and tuned in. Not "I am going to help you!" But rather "How can I help?"

Is it true that sometimes I don't know what I need, and that someone else might? Of course. But if that person were to step in and execute, this would rob me of my own discovery, which is integral to healing and to growth.

If you are always in relationships where you "save others" this is not healthy.

It's called co-dependency.

Relationships don't need a savior and someone who is helpless and needs to be saved.

We do that for ourselves.

Comebacks

Someone says something awful to you and you just stand there, powerless and hurt.

Then, later that day or the next it comes to you: the just-right poison cocktail of words you should have said to deliver the perfect knock-out verbal punch.

Except that if someone says something mean to me and I think of a lethal slingshot retort and hurl it at them just in time, I feel terrible afterwards.

Every time I have been in possession of the sought-after perfect comeback it makes me feel worse rather than better.

Working on developing them exercises a nasty side of me I would rather never nurture.

Why would I want to get proficient at being cruel?

Just because someone hurts me doesn't mean I have to hurt me too.

You can't regret things you didn't say.

You don't need to apologize or forgive yourself for something you refrained from doing.

You can't feel small if you never deliberately cut yourself down.

This is how I discovered that when things get ugly, the most powerful thing to say is nothing.

Narcissism/Self Love

Let's say I am a cup. I hold the pure, clean water of self love.

When my cup is filled to the brim I know for certain that I have enough, and the filter with which I see myself and others is clear.

This means I don't project my issues onto another, I don't take things personally and make no assumptions. It means I have no need to judge or criticize or gossip.

I lead a peaceful, happy life and soon realize that what makes me even happier is offering up what I have to put in the service of others.

This is *meaning*, at least for me.

Life ebbs and flows and the intent of this service to others begins to shift.

Instead of putting my life in the service of others from love I want someone to think well of me. I want to impress. Or to be loved. Or liked.

I want approval.

My cup springs a leak. Doing things to get another to feel anything is not generous. It's the definition of manipulation.

More to the point, it demands that I overextend myself, compromise myself, agree to things I am not comfortable with.

So, it's also a form of deceit. I am pretending to be something I'm not.

The water in my cup is draining fast.

I need to remember what filled my cup. This water springs from within and despite appearances cannot be found in what others think of me.

Self love is the opposite of selfish. The fuller your cup the clearer you see and the more you can give.

Selfishness comes when your intent is contaminated. When you do things "for others" but really for you.

Narcissism is nowhere on this spectrum. It is a mental disorder.

The cup of a narcissist is broken and cannot contain water so there is a perpetual search from the outside world for adulation and approval.

This search is desperate and insatiable: the more adoration, the bigger the need. There is never enough. There never will be.

A narcissist lacks the ability to care or even see anyone beyond themselves.

Up The Ante

I was at home and my mom was running late.

She called and told me she was expecting someone. Could I please chat with her guest for about 30 minutes until she got home?

I was a teenager, maybe 17. This stranger and I talked about loneliness and meaning and fear and she felt like a friend even thought I'd never met her.

I felt lighter when she left.

It's natural to expect friends to be there for you but it's magnificent to think strangers can have your back too.

This has become a theme in my life. Feeling supported by people I don't know at all, maybe *because* they are strangers and have no skin in the game, no expectations or judgment or disappointment or worry or an urge to "fix" anything.

In gratitude for this generosity I try to do the same for others. Lending my ear to a woman on the bus who looks concerned and wants to talk. Hugging a sobbing stranger in the emergency room. I sat with her and held her hand, no questions asked.

Of course I like the notion of random acts of kindness. But hey.

Let's up the ante. A random act of kindness sounds like drive-by benevolence when we are capable of so much more.

We can present someone with the completely unrandom, targeted gift or our attention, or show of support, or act of courtesy.

I have nothing against a cup of coffee for the person behind you in line but if that person is lonely or disoriented or lost (we are all lonely, disoriented and lost), grab a table and sit down.

Give them your presence, your attendance, your care.

Be there for the people that you love. But be there too for that person you've never met.

Don't do it "to be nice." Do it because your own happiness lurks in giving something valuable to another.

Cheer Up!

Whenever I am feeling not happy, people around me seem perturbed.

"Don't worry," they say. *"Cheer up! Don't be sad! There is no reason to be anxious!*

"Keep busy!"

Or, (aaaargck) *"Everything happens for a reason."*

Perpetual happiness is unnatural.

Every feeling I feel is valid. To reject it, to want it to go away, to struggle against it instead of feeling it, means that I am not honoring myself.

"Keeping busy" or pushing any feeling away is becoming numb to what my body is telling me it needs.

I don't want to create a distraction from myself.

If I feel sad I'm going to be sad. If I'm angry I will sit in that anger until I'm ready to come out.

It's ok to feel afraid. And lonely. And filled with doubt. And regret.

This is how things get processed and figured out.

This is how you grow.

It is an integral part of happiness to accept and welcome ourselves for exactly where we are at.

Overactive Imagination

I got up early this morning to go to yoga and the teacher didn't show up. After loitering in the studio for 20 minutes I trudged back home.

Wow. I thought. In the movies this is when I walk in and find Boyfriend having breakfast with another woman.

Maybe she has long, straight hair and is wearing his shirt.

This thought made me furious.

I stormed into my apartment to find…nothing.

Boyfriend was at work, of course.

As preposterous as this sounds, we all do this to ourselves. We argue with our family and our co-workers and our bosses over what we imagine they could say and activate our wrath and wind ourselves up over conversations or incidents that have only happened in our heads.

We tell ourselves we "need to rehearse", and think of multiple possible (catastrophic) ways a conversation can go.

By the time it actually takes place we approach it defensive, rabid, frothing at the mouth, ready to attack.

I need to get out of my imagination and out of all the hypothetical scenarios I have fabricated and into my real life.

I deserve peace of mind and to expect the best from people around me. That they will listen. That they will understand.

I will expect this not just because it's sane, or because abstaining from a thousand fictional conversations is a less painful way to live, but because it allows me to approach my life and relationships like a creator rather than a destroyer.

Another Example Of
A Spectacular Catastrophe

One way or another, we are all held back by what we believe to be true. We are trapped in the mire of the things we tell ourselves.

To discover why we are trapped, we have to look underneath what we think is the culprit.

And then look underneath again.

What traps us is usually hidden under a belief system that we have always accepted as truth and has therefore become invisible to us.

You need an example, so here it is.

I might say *"Giving my friends everything makes me generous and good. I always give my friends everything, and then everyone takes advantage of me. What a cruel world."*

I believe that what gets me stuck is that the world is a cruel place.

I need look underneath that. If *"everyone is taking advantage of my generosity"* maybe my generosity is something to review.

It's really hard for me to review my generosity. I believe not being generous makes me selfish.

This belief has me stuck.

I need to turn the belief around, because believing this is tangling my relationships and leaving me unhappy and resentful.

My own belief is not working in my favor.

It's important to be generous. Maybe I have to begin by being generous with myself.

This is not selfish: this is the definition of a healthy boundary.

But I can't. I can't let go of giving others everything.

Why?

Because I believe I am not good enough.

If I stop bending to everyone's wishes and whims they will leave me.

Hence I need to begin by believing I am worthy of being loved.

That if I respect myself, those around me will love me anyway, and that if they don't I need to find people who love me for who I am and not because I do everything for them.

Healthier boundaries both create and attract healthy relationships.

I surround myself with people who respect me and understand I am generous and can give what is reasonable and what doesn't compromise me.

Look at the things you believe in that are making you suffer. Turn them every which way. Put them back where they belong.

Don't Bother

A beloved friend of mine is in the middle of a nasty divorce and spends a lot of time thinking about how to get back at him.

She and her closest friends talk badly about him and his behavior, how he wronged her, what a bad person he turned out to be.

He cheated on her.

In her mind, he carries all the blame. She is the victim.

How many times has she been in a similar situation?

How many things in common does he or his behavior have with her past relationships?

I don't mean to imply she is at fault.

What I am saying is that if he carries all of the blame, she carries none of the power.

This same pattern will present itself over and over, because she places the blame on another, which frees her of responsibility and leads to her continuing to do the very same things.

We already know that doing the very same things lead to the same result.

Revenge is bad for a lot of reasons, but one of them is that it forces you to focus your energy on another instead of on yourself.

I would much rather she turn her attention on identifying what she needs to do differently so that she never has to go through something like this again.

How To Be A Good Stepmother

Understand that the father of the children will (or should) always put them first. You should aid in this very difficult imperative rather than trying to compete.

In other words, when you fight about the kids, be on the side of the kids, not on your own side.

I know this sounds like it would be to your own detriment, and often it will.

This is long term thinking and the only way to protect your family.

In this relationship (stepmother-kids), you set the tone. If you come in anxious, nervous, worried, or determined to make your voice heard, the kids will respond in kind.

If you come in relaxed, receptive, open, willing to meet them where they are at without pushing or forcing anything then even if the kids don't immediately feel receptive to you, they will come around.

In a very real way you are taking their mother's place. This might make them feel that just by getting along with you they are betraying her. You need to be patient and never position yourself as "another mom."

You're not.

Just for the sake of clarity no matter what you do or what you say or what an angel you are you are not their mother.

You are not their friend. You are not supposed to be.

Please never use the kids as a go-between, to vent or as a source of information. If you want to know anything about your boyfriend, ask him. If something he does bothers you, tell him. Leave the kids out of fights between you and their Dad.

The children will look up to you because they are kids and you are an adult. Because of your place in the family you are an authority figure. This does not mean you can tell them what to do, scold them or boss them around, but you can and should set boundaries. Step firmly into that. Kids like boundaries. It shows them where they stand.

Be there for them. Love them. If you can and you find this in your heart, love them no matter what. You are a parent. Not their mom. Not their Dad. Your own kind of parent.

These kids are about to become your family.

Just to make this extra clear, these kids are about to become your family even if your relationship with their Dad doesn't work out. Follow through with what that means.

Be direct and honest about your opinions. Maybe not explicit—they are kids. But kids respect being treated and talked to like adults.

What you are about to get into is hard. Really hard. You are stepping in the middle of a family that has been broken. Emotions run high. Blame is easy. Things are muddy and murky and complicated and painful.

Learn right now not to take anything personally.

I can't think of any experience—aside from becoming a parent—that will demand more of you or more thoroughly make you a better person.

Maybe It's Not About You

I'm driving through traffic. Someone cuts me off. I am furious, feel attacked. I chase this other car down. I quickly catch up to the offender and see through the window not a vicious monster but someone dancing to music, distracted, oblivious.

Maybe he was driving irresponsibly but he was most definitely not trying to cause me injury.

I arrive at my office. I walk in and say hello to the person sitting at the reception desk. She turns her head away and does not reply.

I spend the morning wondering why she might be angry at me.

Maybe she doesn't like me.

I find out later she was wearing headphones and didn't hear me.

I call a friend and leave yet another voice mail. I wonder why he hasn't called me back. Clearly our relationship is not as important to him as it is to me. This fills me with sadness.

Suddenly I remember: he was going on a camping trip and has no cell phone access.

Taking things personally means interpreting that the actions of another are in relation to us when most of the time things that hurt us, insult us or worry us have nothing to do with us.

Not taking things personally means we make room for the possibility that not everything is about us.

This does not mean that things that aren't personal don't affect us, because they do. It means that we take the blow differently because our emotions are not all wrapped up in what happened.

This is important because by setting our ego aside we fight less, get angry less, feel offended less, suffer less.

Rumination

I used to play events over and over in my head. I believed that if I did, I could fix things.

I could fix things if I went over them enough.

I could control the future too if I could play it out in my brain. If I went over every step of how my day was going to go I would be efficient and fast and not forget anything and even be ready for disaster.

I got really good at ruminating because I practiced it for years.

Now, when my brain wants to do this I remind myself it's obsessive behavior and not actually constructive.

I can't either fix or control anything. At least not with my thoughts.

I replace rumination with focusing on my breath.

At first it's incredibly difficult because I have practiced the other behavior for so long. I am in effect attempting to break a habit I spent years building so now it's resilient and strong.

Just because a habit is bad doesn't mean it was not built well.

As time goes by, pushing through "this is really difficult" ultimately reduces my tendency to go over things in this busy, restless, nervous brain and quiet it down.

It's Me I'm Angry At

Resentment is what I feel when I put someone's desires before my own in an effort to please or get another to think highly of me.

If the gesture comes from a place of generosity I feel happy, balanced.

If it comes from failing to represent myself I feel bitter and angry.

Resentment is a symptom of poor boundaries.

It comes disguised as me feeling anger towards another person, but I know better.

It's really me being angry at myself for not standing up for what I want, like, need or prefer.

It's what happens when I am not true to myself.

Incompatible

I had heard enough about Burning Man to know I would never be interested in going.

That's an understatement.

I knew there was no force on Earth powerful enough to make me go.

Then I started dating a guy who distracted me with many, many things I am completely distracted by, like his salt and pepper hair and scratchy beard and big nose.

Next thing I knew I was packing.

Baby wipes, because I would be unable to shower. Clothes and boots I wouldn't mind ruining forever. Ear plugs to protect me from relentless noise.

Why? Why was I doing this to myself? Why was I putting myself in an impossible position? Why was I jeopardizing what this relationship could become?

Why? Why? Why? Why?

bangs forehead against table

Burning Man was one of the best experiences of my life.

There are two types of incompatibility.

The first feels to me like I'm swimming against a powerful current. It's difficult and counterintuitive and exhausting and frustrating and terrifying and tests me and the limits of my patience and sanity.

It can feel pretty awful.

But on the other end it's gratifying and life-affirming because it expands me.

What would happen to me and to my life if what I did was limited to what I prefer?

I would shrink to the point of oblivion.

I don't know what I want or what I like because how come that open desert was so heart-filling?

The second type of incompatibility feels to me like a concrete wall, unscalable and impossible to negotiate. I can't do that. It doesn't expand me. It diminishes me, compromises me, and that will never do.

The catch is that sometimes it takes time to determine which type of incompatibility you are dealing with, and this nobody can help you with.

The only person who can make this distinction is you.

Change The Record

We say negative things to ourselves all day long, even when at some level we know they can't all possibly be true.

"Oh my god you are a disaster a loser a fool you're not good enough don't say that don't do that don't act that way don't wear that you look like an idiot you don't deserve anything good —"

Positive affirmations are not meant for you to believe. They are meant to change the same old record playing in your head.

They are meant to counteract the incredible damage you do to yourself with that perpetual, relentless self-attack.

Then, after some time, on a day when you are too distracted or too tired to defend yourself against someone who compliments you, a bit of the positive may seep in at a moment when you are receptive to believe it.

"Maybe I can do this."

This might only sink in for a fraction of a second.

And yet a teeny, tiny, minuscule bit of light can combat a whole lot of darkness.

When I Was Thirteen

When I was thirteen and had a boyfriend and he said he didn't like me anymore *"oh my god no problem just tell me what you like and I'll be that and then you can like me again this can be fixed."*

Changing in order for someone else to like me doesn't work. It never will, and learning that lesson at 13 might have meant I would not have to learn it at 23, and 33, and later.

When he said no thank you this is not about you changing, I thought *"That's it my life is over I will never ever love again."*

Breaking up with a guy doesn't mean I'm finished, it doesn't mean that by far, and understanding this at thirteen might have made things easier for what came after.

Nothing is finished, it's just the beginning. You are just getting started and it doesn't matter how old you are.

It was good at thirteen to drown my feelings in some delicious spoonful of something creamy and sweet, but there are better things than teaching myself to search for solace and comfort in food.

I would have liked to try a rock climbing class instead, to surprise myself with my own capabilities, to grab a tiny ledge and pull myself, pull myself up.

I will always be able to pull myself up.

I would have liked to try a boxing class to punch something, to hit something, to kick something in a place where doing those things was encouraged.

I want my anger to find its rightful place and tell me what I need to hear.

Your anger wants to tell you something but it takes years for you to hear it because *no, no don't be angry anger is ugly and better kept away.*

Please be angry. Please be sad. These are your feelings and because they are yours, a part of you, they are integral to what makes you beautiful and capable and whole.

Later Will Be Better

I am sitting cross-legged on a wooden floor trying to meditate.

I am feeling pretty uncomfortable. I think I would be able to do this better if I could switch the cross of my legs.

I switch the cross of my legs.

A corner of my eye itches. I will scratch it. I will scratch it and then peace and I will be one.

I scratch it, and as I do my head itches, and my nose. I twitch around.

My brain is just as unsettled. I begin to go over all the things I need to do right after my meditation.

Come back. Come back to your breath but I can't yes you can come back.

I want to stretch out my neck. I want to stretch out my neck and then silence will be mine.

This is how I learn that I have now. I need to meet it all as it is —my restlessness and itchiness and my fidgety, fidgety nature.

I need to sit in joy and pleasure and discomfort and pain and itchiness.

It will not be better later. I will never be perfectly comfortable and as such the time to be perfectly still is now.

Life is just like this. Things will be perfect just as soon as I figure out what I want. When I lose five pounds and let my hair grow long and find a boyfriend and learn to bake a perfect cake and get another job.

Life would be perfect if only I didn't feel so lost.

But the belief that happiness is somewhere else, after somewhere else, as soon as you do whatever, is a distraction—a decoy—from what you have to put in order within yourself.

Accept now. Find happiness now. It's all we've got.

Vulnerability/Neediness

Neediness is the belief that someone else can satiate an inner hunger before realizing that any inner hunger can only be quenched by working on yourself.

Being vulnerable is opening yourself up to getting hurt, most commonly after recognizing that getting hurt is not something that can ever be avoided.

How To Be Sure You Are Marrying The Right Person

I recently bought a sweater I was sure I'd wear every day and it's sitting in my closet, untouched.

No matter how much I think about what I buy, I really have not been able to accurately predict what I will end up using.

Sometimes I will buy something both nonsensical and impractical and end up pulling it out almost every day.

I am sitting at the airport waiting for my flight to be announced. I can't be sure the plane will leave on time or leave at all.

When I pick a career or a job I think it's good and I think I will like it but what if my tastes change?

How likely is it that in five, ten years I will develop other interests that today I cannot foresee?

If I can't figure out my closet, I guess I can forget about more complicated things.

When I find someone I believe I want to spend the rest of my life with, or even a weekend with, there is no way to know for sure my choice will be the right one.

I just had a bunch of medical tests done and I thought I was healthy but I couldn't be sure.

What I learned is that I can't even know what is happening inside my own body, even if I inhabit it every day.

The only thing I can be sure of is my ability to successfully handle life when it goes in a direction I did not expect.

I can also be certain that life will, without fail, behave unpredictably.

I know this sounds scary at first.

My hope is that as you get used to the fact that there are no guarantees, you can begin to appreciate life for the adventure that it is.

Echo Chambers

When we get up in the morning and turn on music we pick what we want to listen to and don't need to listen to anything else.

We move through our day averting our eyes if we come across something we don't want to see, then pay no attention to anyone who doesn't think the way we do.

We choose to hang out with people like us and click on stories that interest us so that the engines that we use (social media channels, news organizations, search) learn what to show us.

We shop for books and clothes on sites who can then say "people who bought these things also bought these." Like-minded people. Not those who might have a different taste or style.

We meet relationship prospects and choose those compatible to us and we consider being similar a prize.

"We are perfectly compatible," we say. *"Perfect for each other."*

We watch movies about things we are already interested in and go to dinner to restaurants where they serve food we like.

We go to rallies to be convinced of all the things we already believe in.

This ability to turn our lives into echo chambers closes us off to seeing something differently.

Real Threat

I don't worry about incompatibility or fights or lovers.

I can see those coming. Hoofs that sound like thunder.

I worry about television.

You and your significant other leave the house and go through two completely different experiences.

When you come home, *"Tell me about your day"* sounds a bit like *"Let's bring back everything you found difficult or frustrating."*

So instead, you sit and watch something on television.

Sitting in front of the TV lulls you into feeling you are doing something together but wake up. You might be sitting together but you are watching alone.

Your brain is not even on.

The next night, your time together shrinks.

"Let's hurry up and have dinner so we can watch our show."

You make it sound like a form of complicity but it's just the opposite. Soon you are not connecting. You are sacrificing coming together in the communion of a family meal in exchange for a cold, flickering blue light.

Then you wonder why you feel so distant, so isolated and alone.

Let's get rid of the television. It doesn't matter what happens. Before you know it you have given hours to a show that will suffer through a badly written season and the fate of your characters won't be worth watching anyway.

Turn to look at your significant other. Maybe instead of asking about his day go for a walk or snuggle or make love or go to dinner or pull anything out of the fridge and sit at the dining room table.

Do it now, before you look back and realize he has become a roommate, an acquaintance, a stranger.

A Storm Is Coming

Your life is like a ship.

You travel across oceans exploring, gathering experience and knowledge, taking risks.

You set down anchor to gather yourself for the next journey.

This is when you course-correct, undergo repairs and restoration, get stronger.

Making your ship better or different for someone other than yourself is like securing your anchor onto something that appears to be but is not immovable weight.

You think you are held firmly in place but you instead will drift.

Bad or good, the changes you make won't take.

Change for you. Grow for you. Impress yourself. There will be storms to weather.

The work you do on this ship will alter the course of your life. You cannot afford transient adjustments.

Distant Planets

Boyfriend works about an hour away from where we live.

We typically spend a lot of time together over the weekend, and not a lot of time together through the week.

Sometimes when he leaves for work on Monday morning I feel a pang of separation anxiety.

Me: *"Good bye. I love you. You meant so much to me!"*

Him: *"Dushka. I will see you tonight."*

I have explained to him how his Monday morning departure makes me feel and he claims it's nonsensical.

Which of course it is.

But I'm describing a *feeling*, and he's countering with *reason*.

That's two different planets.

We've learned to respect each of our planets for what it is.

A feeling is the full responsibility of the person feeling it and cannot expect or demand that another person accommodate it.

But it doesn't have to be right, cannot be wrong, and doesn't respond to being reasoned with.

It just is.

Me: *"Goodbye! Farewell! Safe travels!"*

Him: *Hugs me extra tight. Understands me. Exits.*

Remind Yourself

When I find myself trying to control another person:

I remind myself that I don't want to be nosy, pushy, insistent, invasive or suspicious.

More than anything, I want to handle things with grace. It has a much better aftertaste than seeing myself turn into a nag.

I regard another person's behavior as a gift—something meant to teach me. This helps me approach situations from a place of gratitude rather than anger.

I remind myself to stay in the now. No "what ifs" or hypothetical scenarios or conversations that only happen in my head.

I think less, obsess less, and focus on my breath more. Inhale. Exhale.

I develop, explore and nurture my own interests and my own pursuits. I don't need another person to feel "complete."

I support the people that I love without self interest. No pushing. No manipulating a certain outcome. What I push pushes me back. Things cannot be forced.

I open my heart and assume that whatever happens will happen in my best interest. I don't believe the universe conspires in my favor. I live my life as if it did because it has a transformative effect on how I operate and how things affect me.

I put another person's feelings before my own in an effort to develop compassion. It feels better than being perpetually resentful.

I make an effort to recognize and discard anything motivated by my ego. She can get pretty big.

I consider what I could be doing for others rather than living at the mercy of my internal storms.

I assume others have the best intentions.

Maybe they don't but I really don't want to expend any energy walking around being suspicious of everyone. This does not protect me. It diminishes me.

My Indestructible Heart

You probably already know the heart is a muscle.

You can run and make it stronger but staying contributes to its resilience too.

So go ahead and get disappointed. Feel sad. Be hungry, so hungry for affection it hurts.

Love someone. Love someone madly, so much it aches, and then see that person leave you, maybe for someone else.

Feel your heart break.

Be a witness to death and realize no one you love can escape it.

Grow old enough to see clearly that you will lose everything, everything that matters, and that those most important to you will one day lose you.

Now feel your heart again, glorious and muscular and full of your sinew and your blood, intact.

Your heart will still work like new if you let it.

A heart, regardless of its current state is the best thing in the world to own. Mine is indestructible and so is yours.

Everyone's Fine

My parents were both extremely apprehensive. They wanted to make sure no harm ever befell me and had a tendency to be both overprotective and dramatic.

To them, the whole world was fraught with peril.

This is how I learned that worry = love.

In my own relationships if I fell in love with someone I fretted constantly about his well-being.

"Oh my god—be careful! Drive slowly! Call me when you get there! Let me know what time you get home! Any team sport sounds like a terrible idea! Why can't you just take up playing chess? Why can't you just read?"

For me, I was taking care of him. You know, loving him.

For him, I was suffocating him.

It took me a long time to separate loving someone from worrying about them.

You know what? Capable, independent adults feel not only smothered but even insulted by another person assuming they need taking care of.

They will drive carefully as an act of intelligence and self-preservation and don't need a pesky curly haired individual on high alert constantly attempting to improve their behavior.

I had no idea what it was that others could possibly find so irritating.

I had to take a good look at myself and identify how on top of everything else worrying about everything accomplished nothing.

(Also, I was utterly exhausted by all the people who needed protecting.)

Once I pinpointed this (*Whoa! I am so annoying!*) I had to go even deeper than that to analyze my definition of love.

I had to notice how becoming someone who didn't worry could not happen until I untangled "worry" from "love."

In my brain, not worrying meant not loving, so not worrying felt counterintuitive; almost like by not worrying I was putting the people that I loved in danger.

But, no.

I worry a lot less, interfere a lot less and focus only on taking care of myself. Incredibly, everyone seems to be doing just fine.

Tease

When I was in junior high school a handful of girls had a reputation for being *calientahuevos*.

The meaning of this expression is similar to "being a tease."

The literal translation is "testicle warmer."

It's the girl willing to go pretty far but who stops short of engaging in full sexual intercourse.

The implication is that if you are going to make out then you are expected to go all the way.

Like, lest he get "blue balls", you owe it to him.

This is a horrific mindset because it takes away consent.

A woman is the owner of her body.

This means I can kiss you and not want to make out; make out and not want to have sex; have sex and not want to have sex again.

Saying no at any point is my right and anyone overriding it is committing sexual abuse.

If a girl says no and you are under the impression she can't say no because she has already done this much—or has already had sex with you in the past, or is your girlfriend—and push her into having sex, this is the very definition of rape.

Just because behavior is culturally accepted doesn't make it right.

Time Is Running Out

I am having dinner with a friend who is saying she has not found a significant other and is running out of time.

She's in her early thirties.

I can understand why she feels this way but the fact is she has all the time in the world.

Her believing time is running out makes her come at this from a place of anxiety, tension, desperation.

"Why don't you try online dating?" I say.

"Because I will not find what I am looking for that way."

She is defeated. She is defeated, and she has not begun.

"Why not?"

"Because I've tried it before and it didn't work."

Is trying something and failing an indication it will never work?

Is there no value in trying again? Isn't perseverance the key to success?

"I want to be chosen," she says. *"I want someone to look at me across a crowded room."*

We all want the dream.

But fairy tales are fantasy, and fantasy, meant to inspire, can instead lead to paralysis.

You can't wait for dreams to come true. You have to create them.

My friend is clear on what she wants but has convinced herself that to find it she can't do a thing.

Good Questions To Ask The First Time You Meet Someone

What do you do on Sunday afternoons?

What are you reading?

Who do you miss?

When was the last time you lied?

Would you take the first train going anywhere?

Thoreau says we all live lives of quiet desperation. Do you agree?

Do you like your job?

How many really good friends do you have?

Do you get along with your exes?

Where did you go on your last trip?

What would you do if money was not an issue?

And of course—before we go any further, do you love me?

Hehehehe.

Just kidding on the last one.

Listen To Your Feelings

Imagine that I am walking down the street, step on uneven pavement and twist my ankle.

"Keep walking," my brain says. *"Just keep walking."*

"But, what if I hurt myself and walking makes it worse?" my brain asks. *"Maybe we should stop."*

These are thoughts. And as it often happens, they are contradictory thoughts.

That's not helpful.

What am I feeling?

I feel like maybe I should take my shoe off and look at my ankle.

Wait. That's also a thought. What am I *feeling*?

Owww. Pain is a feeling. A flare of anger at my carelessness. Concern.

My ankle really hurts.

What should I do next? I know it sounds logical, reasonable, to follow my thoughts. But they are yanking me around. They can't make up their mind.

My ankle is throbbing. As inconvenient as that is, as much as I don't want it to hurt, I don't care what I think. I care what I feel.

I request that my thoughts pull themselves together and figure out a way to get me to a place where I can get my ankle checked.

I cannot allow my thoughts to command me. I am not saying my feelings should command me.

I am saying I am the boss, and after I listen to my often dissenting voices I get to decide the best course of action.

Don't Work Too Hard

Imagine for a moment that I am aboard a big ship in the middle of the ocean. I fall off this ship into the choppy waters below.

I'm a decent swimmer, despite of which I begin to thrash. I thrash because I'm terrified. I fell off a ship, cannot see land, and don't know what else is in the water.

I am unlikely to make it if I keep thrashing. Thrashing is ineffective and expends energy that I should be trying to conserve. I could be wading way more slowly, in a more coordinated way. I could even be mostly floating.

Which is to say maximum effort does not equal maximum results.

My life sometimes feels like I have fallen off a ship in the middle of the ocean, and I indeed thrash around a lot. In small and big ways I work harder than I need to.

I wake up with a tense jaw because I have been gnashing my teeth while I sleep. At the end of the day I frequently have pain on my shoulders even when I don't remember using them for anything.

I clench my jaws when I hold imaginary arguments with people.

Imaginary arguments. About things that haven't happened.

Sometimes it takes me twenty sentences to explain what I could tell you in six and I fret about things I have no control over—at least not through fretting.

I intensely partake in wishful thinking instead of preparedness and mistrust people to do what they tell me they are going to do.

Trusting is liberating.

I have resolved to be more vigilant about the ways I work harder than I have to, not so much because I want to work less but because I need every ounce of power applied to places where my effort is more likely to count.

Pedestal

Exalting someone is the opposite of flattering. It's a form of distortion.

It's uncomfortable because the things another claims to love do not coincide with who you are.

Idealizing someone is less like admiration and more like confusing the person you idealize with somebody else.

Are You The One Who Is Toxic?

The most frequent symptom that you are the person giving you the most trouble is the sense that *everyone* wrongs you.

You often wonder why everyone is so horrible, why all your friends betray you, why nobody understands you, why everyone you date sucks, why there are no good men (or women) out there anymore.

One day you realize, exhausted, that you really don't want to do this anymore and that you will have to put up with yourself forever unless you fix this.

And that the single common denominator that all these awful people that you somehow end up in relationships with have is you.

And that's how you know.

Trust Is For You

When you decide to forgive someone you realize that forgiveness is not something you grant another person but a gift you give yourself.

Forgiveness is putting down something that burdens you.

It does not mean you have to pretend the transgression never happened or that you have to welcome the transgressor into your life.

It just means you are not carrying anything heavy around anymore.

Trust is similar.

As you become stronger, as your mind becomes clearer, as you become braver, you learn to trust yourself.

You trust that you will be able to successfully deal with any situation and as such decide to live free of the shackles of suspicion, the burden that is the constant anticipation that another person will eventually hurt you.

Trust, like forgiveness, is unrelated to others. It's a more freeing, lighter way of life you choose for yourself.

Why Do We Make Life Complicated?

We complicate life in large part because we feel the need to react immediately to what we hear, see or feel.

So much of what complicates my life comes from convincing myself rushing is better than pausing.

"Take a breath, Dushka."

I try to give myself a pause between what causes me to want to react and the reaction itself.

This alone has made my life a whole lot simpler.

You Don't Have To Live Like This

I have suffered from lower back pain for most of my life.

While seldom incapacitating, it has been ever-present. I sleep face up with a pillow under my knees, get up early and in pain (staying in bed too long makes it worse), and push through the first 15 minutes of any yoga class to get myself to a point where I begin to feel more mobile.

I have been practicing yoga for about six years and in that time the pain has gotten better but has never disappeared.

I got certified to be a yoga teacher and learned, among other things, the meaning of proper alignment and how that is different for every body. I followed that certification with a yoga therapeutics course to better understand structure and function.

In the course of this year I have been hearing about the body and about injuries and have been talking to patients.

I can't believe it took so long for a very fundamental thing to finally get through to me.

I don't need to live like this.

I don't have to be in pain.

The fact that the pain is something I can withstand does not make it OK.

This morning I went to see a physical therapist, the same one who taught the yoga therapeutics course.

He talked to me and examined me for over an hour. It turns out I have structural issues: scoliosis of the spine, one of my legs is longer than the other and as such bears much of my weight, my sacroiliac joint was out of place.

With proper care, I can get better.

This is what I learned: We are survivors.

There is a lot we get used to, often inadvertently. We begin by feeling discomfort or pain and slowly, over the years, we fail to notice or regard it as normal.

I am, of course, not only talking about the body.

No form of discomfort is normal. Pain is not normal. Having to limit ourselves and not do things we should be able to do is not normal.

We should strive to get better. At least we should try.

Regret

We all want to live a life free of pain. A life free of mistakes. A life free of regrets.

Except that everything that makes life worth living—love and joy and learning and understanding and growth—every beautiful thing is intertwined, inextricable, from these things.

You can't avoid these but if you somehow figured out how, you would be cheating yourself out of everything.

Ego/Self-Esteem

If I love someone and they tell me they don't love me, I realize that them not loving me does not make me less worthy of being loved.

Me not being loved by another might hurt my feelings but it does not impact my self-esteem.

This is because self-esteem is how I see myself, and it comes from inside me.

Ego is a ravenous search for external validation.

We all have an ego. It is part of our composition. But sometimes it gets out of control.

An out of control ego must be an expert at everything, does not accept ever being wrong, shows off, needs to be the best, is convinced the problem is everybody else, finds it difficult to apologize, regards everything as a competition and has to win.

A person with a healthy self-esteem is happy to learn from others, sees herself clearly and does not link being right or winning with her self worth.

The relationship between ego and self-esteem is inversely proportional.

Expectations

Living a life with expectations means you see things as you want them to be rather than as they are.

I don't think it's possible to live a life without expectations.

What's possible is to create an awareness that I have them so I can make a distinction between what I want and who people are.

This way I can identify that it's not others disappointing me but rather that I'm disappointing myself.

The result is healthier relationships.

Why Does No Mean Yes?

When I was growing up in Mexico men having sex were displaying virility and prowess and women having sex were sluts.

This put women in a position where they needed to pretend they didn't want sex and played coy and said no when they really wanted to say yes.

This put men in a position to assume no could mean yes if they pushed.

I don't mean to imply that this is women's fault or men's fault.

I mean to imply this is a vicious circle that muddles communication and makes consent something you have to interpret.

This is fertile ground for sexual assault.

Pop culture perpetuates this. The woman says no. The man pushes. The woman succumbs. We sigh.

Consider the first time Han Solo kisses Princess Leia.

She clearly and quite aggressively pushes him away. She says no. She says no again. She shakes her head.

He kisses her.

We think it's romantic.

No wonder we are confused.

What if we remove the game playing?

Women would have to admit to liking sex as much as men like sex (and I do).

Then, the initiator would say something along the lines of *"I'd like to kiss you. Is that OK?"*

If I said no that would mean he would understand, take a step back and not kiss me.

I could not afford to take this risk if I really did want him to kiss me, so I'd say yes.

We would live in a world where no would mean no, and yes would mean yes.

If anyone thinks this is in any way less romantic let me tell you there is nothing as dreamy as the truth, nothing as healthy as clear boundaries and nothing as conducive to good sex as clear communication.

My Internal Ocean

My most favorite part of a beach vacation is that moment where you walk onto the sand and take off your shoes and look out into the water and breathe in the ocean air. That first overwhelming, chest-expanding feeling of "here I am."

So, there I was.

I lay down my towel and knelt on it and took a few things out of my beach bag. Sunscreen, another towel, a pile of books.

That's when a big wave drenched everything.

I was angry at first *"EVERYTHING IS WET YOU STUPID, STUPID OCEAN YOU HAVE NO RIGHT TO DO THIS TO ME!"*

Then of course I realized being angry at a force of nature was neither useful or effective.

More importantly, I was missing the whole point of its magnificence.

I set aside all my (soaking, maybe ruined) things and took my t-shirt off and waded right into the next wave.

I bobbed up and down in the clear blue water.

Very quickly I went from massively inconvenienced to the luckiest person in the world, to get to be here, experiencing this.

My feelings are an internal ocean. I can't control them. I can disapprove of them or try to push them away but I quickly find they are much bigger than me.

I now go ahead and wade in. It takes some courage and the first sensation might be one of shock, but I quickly realize it's the only place to be.

The view from in here is magnificent.

Happy Doesn't Just Happen

To me, the word "ferocious" implies tenacity and verve and grit.

Happy is something I strive to be. It doesn't just happen to me. I think about it, I adjust my perspective and (attempt to) learn painful lessons and am sometimes miserable and figure out how to get out of that misery and try again.

I've come to the conclusion that *happy* is a word associated more to meaning than it is to pleasure. It's more about discomfort and learning and devotion and gratitude than about laughter, a sunny day and a slice of cake covered with rainbow sprinkles. (Although I welcome any of these highly perishable things.)

I am ferociously happy. Within that utter happiness I accept the frequent presence of anxiety and grief and sadness and anger and frustration and fear and honor all these visitors as part of the deal I have struck. Yes. Yes to everything.

How Important Is A Partner With Ambition?

The word "ambition" is tricky territory.

On the one hand it conveys search and aspiration and drive and motivation and desire and life.

Who doesn't want that?

On the other, it speaks of selfishness and murky values.

Like charisma that carries a knife.

I don't like scheming or aggression, taking every careful step by design, a combative spirit that turns everything into a competition.

A cutthroat attitude is shortsighted and I prefer vision.

I do love a partner with an appetite. I admire ardor and energy and enterprise. I relate to hunger and yearning. The opposite would be apathy and maybe even indifference.

I would find the absence of longing hard to live with.

Farmer's Market

I am a lover of food in all its glorious bounty and have a tendency to overdo it.

Some days I really feel like my system could use a break.

I can absolutely relate to the sensation of wanting to fast.

It's just that fasting doesn't work for me. I need to eat. If I resolve to abstain from eating, by 9:20 a.m. on that day I have a headache and feel ravenous enough to tip the contents of the refrigerator into my mouth.

I don't handle deprivation very well.

One day, feeling lethargic and bleh, I decided what I craved was vegetable soup.

I went to the Farmer's Market and found every vegetable that looked colorful, crispy, happy and in season.

Onions, carrots, celery, kale, spinach, mushrooms, sweet potatoes (they are not a vegetable but yes to sweet potatoes), broccoli, cauliflower, anything.

Then, I came home, chopped it all up and created a gigantic pot of vegetable soup. When it was ready, I generously squeezed lime juice across the top.

Over the next few days I ate it when I felt like it. Sometimes for breakfast, but most often for dinner. When I wasn't eating my soup I tried eating light—scrambled eggs, a salad, grilled chicken or fish.

This has become my personal tradition. Whenever I realize I have been eagerly devouring too many cookies and macaroons and am starting to feel sluggish, heavy or high on sugar, I make a trip to the Farmer's Market.

Toxic Relationships Can Be Turned Around

When I first met Boyfriend our relationship was fiery and difficult. We are both quirky, headstrong and set in our ways.

When things were going well everything ran fast and smooth like a car zooming around a racetrack. When things went haywire that car caught on something imperceptible, flipped over and was engulfed in flames.

Our fights were cataclysmic.

Let me give you an example.

I am the oldest of many siblings and was raised being told taking care of them was my responsibility.

I check in on the people that I love and provide commentary on what they are doing. *"Call me when you get there and don't forget your sweater"* is how I show love.

Boyfriend was the youngest boy in a family with an apprehensive mom and two older sisters. Being checked in on and "told what to do" freaks him out. He detests it.

How I show love lines up with what makes him run.

I have dozens of examples like this, where our panic buttons were accidentally activated with precision and accuracy by the very nature of the other person.

Our relationship was not only potentially toxic but combustible. It threatened to self destruct by the time you finished reading this paragraph.

And yet, here we are.

I believe a toxic relationship can be turned around. But you need to be willing to look at yourself and take responsibility.

To not only stop doing what you are doing but understand why.

To be open to reconsider your definition of love and how you express it.

The reward is not just a healthier relationship with the person that you love but a healthier relationship with everyone, because changing your patterns rewrites every tacit rule you ever established.

For some time we went to couples counseling. Our therapist told us we often choose the people who push our buttons because as adults we have the power to address and resolve what once hurt us.

If you put in the work, love will heal you.

Nobody Cares

A friend of mine recently published a book and called me frantic because the response to this book wasn't what he expected.

Why wasn't anyone paying attention? Why wasn't it selling? Why wasn't he getting showered with extraordinary, thoughtfully written, touching reviews?

Because, I said, nobody cares.

Writing a book is like a friend inviting you over to see a slide show of his family's vacation photos.

I mean, you truly love him and his kids but, really? Must we?

Writing a book very, very rarely results in fame or attention.

It's instead a lesson in humility.

It costs more to create than what you get in royalties—you'd have to be a star to come out even.

When it comes to any form of art—painting, sculpture, writing—you do it because you love it. Because you have to. Because it brings you pleasure.

Because the process teaches you something invaluable (among other things, to check your ego at the door).

I highly recommend writing a book. What I want is for you to do it for the right reasons so that you enjoy the process rather than suffer through it.

If your motivation is external, such as approval, attention, admiration or money, chances are you are in for a painful and disappointing ride.

Go Make Something

I once met a man who, disenchanted with his job and feeling like nothing he did mattered, decided to leave and make something.

Instead of being stuck behind a computer he would go outside into the sun and build something with his hands.

He spent his annual salary on the creation of a monumental sculpture.

He transported this art piece to a dry lake bed in the middle of the Nevada desert.

People came from all over the world to see it, and then one early morning, before the sun came up, he burned it down.

How could he feel listless working in a cubicle, and feel so good making something, only to obliterate it?

Making things is life expressing itself.

Spiders make cobwebs. Beavers make dams.

Humans make families and books and sculpture and painting.

We make music and scarves and cookies and doodles and meals and clothes.

We spin stories.

Making things switches on a sense of purpose and makes us feel a fundamental thing: that we are *useful*.

It's a primordial command and it plugs us into a splendid element within ourselves.

Then, it connects us to others.

To me, it has a bit to do with legacy and what you will leave behind, but mostly making something is necessary to happiness and is its own reward.

Your Puzzle

Imagine you go to a toy store and buy the biggest, most beautiful puzzle you can find.

You want to go home, assemble it and hang it on your wall.

That's when you spot another big, beautiful puzzle. You decide to take that home too.

If you go home and open up both boxes and mix all the small, elaborate pieces into one big pile, it will be so much harder to figure out which piece goes where.

And yet this is what we do to our relationships.

We each need the space, time and dedication to work on our own puzzle to then stand next to another able to offer a clearer, more complete image of who we are.

Morning Person

I used to be nocturnal.

I had a column in *El Universal*, a newspaper in Mexico City, and I wrote at night.

I loved it, the silence, the light of the moon and that sense that nights belonged only to me.

How it felt like I was stepping out of time.

It had a romance too, its own allure, the sleep deprivation, looking haggard.

Like writing had a price that I was willing to pay.

I feared that what I found in the night would never be available to me in the harsh, white light of day.

One (late) morning I decided that writing was a gift rather than a sacrifice. A joy, intended to delight me. Something to do with love.

It has no price.

Now I want to be at my best to receive it, at my most resilient and expansive, healthy and well rested.

I get up early to make time to write and sit at a sunny table near a window.

I make this special place for it but tell us both every day that it's not sacred. As proof, I write everywhere. In coffee shops, on the bus, while I wait in line, during commercial breaks.

Invite your creativity everywhere. Don't ask it if it wants to come—just make space and wave it in. It might take a while for it to adjust to its new surroundings. It might need informal coaxing. But it will come.

The last thing you want to do is persuade something tenacious that it's fragile.

My creativity is mine, an inherent part of me, indivisible. It's not like it can go anywhere. It has gloss and lust and muscle; it's diurnal now, sturdy, ambulatory, itinerant, free.

About the Author

After more than 20 years in the communications industry I noticed a theme.

It is very difficult to articulate who you are and what you do.

This holds true for both companies and for individuals.

For companies, this is an impediment to the development of an identity, a reputation, a brand.

It makes it hard for your customers to see how you are different from your competitors.

For individuals, in a new world order of personal brands, it makes it hard to develop one that feels real.

This is what I do. I help companies and people put into simple terms who they are, what they do, and where to go next.

My work comes to life through message development, presentation training, media training and personal brand development.

It comes to life through executive coaching, workshops and public speaking.

It comes to life through what I write.

I live in San Francisco with Boyfriend, who after five years still makes me coffee every morning.

Printed in Poland
by Amazon Fulfillment
Poland Sp. z o.o., Wrocław